THE UNUTTE

D0339171

Books by

G. A. STUDDERT KENNEDY

The New Man in Christ
Food for the Fed-up
The Warrior, the Woman and the Christ
Rhymes
Lies
The Wicket Gate
The Unutterable Beauty

and his

Memoir by his Friends

THE
UNUTTERABLE
BEAUTY

G. A. STUDDERT KENNEDY

HODDER AND STOUGHTON

This book was first published in 1927, and since then has been constantly reprinted, both under its original title *The Unutterable Beauty* and, in the famous "Black Jacket" series, under the title *The Rhymes of G. A. Studdert Kennedy*.

First paperback edition 1964
Second impression 1968

SBN 340 01842 9

Printed and bound in Great Britain for Hodder and Stoughton Ltd, St Paul's House, Warwick Lane, London E.C.4, by Butler and Tanner Ltd, Frome and London

CONDITIONS OF SALE

PUBLISHER'S NOTE

The Rev. G. A. Studdert Kennedy was perhaps the most famous Padre serving in the war of 1914–18. As "Woodbine Willie" he was known all along the Western Front, and the name is a sure indication of the great affection in which he was held by the men who gave it to him. "Woodbine Willie's" *Rough Rhymes of a Padre* moved the hearts of thousands of people in the Great War. They said for the soldiers the things they wanted to say for themselves, and brought home the truth to the people left in England. Since then many thousands of readers have continued to find strength and comfort in his poems and in all his writings. Everything Studdert Kennedy did and wrote bore the marks of a great man, passionate in his tenderness for suffering and striving humanity, fierce in his hatred of hypocrisy and cant. The book published under the title *The Unutterable Beauty* contains all the poems which he himself wished to live.

CONTENTS

DIALECT POEMS

WOODBINE WILLIE

They gave me this name like their nature,
    Compacted of laughter and tears,
A sweet that was born of the bitter,
    A joke that was torn from the years.

Of their travail and torture, Christ's fools,
    Atoning my sins with their blood,
Who grinned in their agony sharing
    The glorious madness of God.

Their name!   Let me hear it — the symbol
    Of unpaid — unpayable debt,
For the men to whom I owed God's Peace,
    I put off with a cigarette.

THE SUFFERING GOD

If He could speak, that victim torn and bleeding,
    Caught in His pain and nailed upon the Cross,
Has He to give the comfort souls are needing?
    Could He destroy the bitterness of loss?

Once and for all men say He came and bore it,
    Once and for all set up His throne on high,
Conquered the world and set His standard o'er it,
    Dying that once, that men might never die.

Yet men are dying, dying soul and body,
    Cursing the God who gave to them their birth,
Sick of the world with all its sham and shoddy,
    Sick of the lies that darken all the earth.

Peace we were pledged, yet blood is ever flowing,
    Where on the earth has Peace been ever found?
Men do but reap the harvest of their sowing,
    Sadly the songs of human reapers sound.

Sad as the winds that sweep across the ocean,
    Telling to earth the sorrow of the sea.
Vain is my strife, just empty idle motion,
    All that has been is all there is to be.

So on the earth the time waves beat in thunder,
    Bearing wrecked hopes upon their heaving breasts,
Bits of dead dreams, and true hearts torn asunder,
    Flecked with red foam upon their crimson crests.

How can it be that God can reign in glory,
    Calmly content with what His Love has done,
Reading unmoved the piteous shameful story,
    All the vile deeds men do beneath the sun?

Are there no tears in the heart of the Eternal?
    Is there no pain to pierce the soul of God?
Then must He be a fiend of Hell infernal,
    Beating the earth to pieces with His rod.

Or is it just that there is nought behind it,
    Nothing but forces purposeless and blind?
Is the last thing, if mortal man could find it,
    Only a power wandering as the wind?

Father, if He, the Christ, were Thy Revealer,
    Truly the First Begotten of the Lord,
Then must Thou be a Suff'rer and a Healer,
    Pierced to the heart by the sorrow of the sword.

Then must it mean, not only that Thy sorrow
   Smote Thee that once upon the lonely tree,
But that to-day, to-night, and on the morrow,
   Still it will come, O Gallant God, to Thee.

Swift to its birth in spite of human scorning
   Hastens the day, the storm-clouds roll apart;
Rings o'er the earth the message of the morning,
   Still on the Cross the Saviour bares His heart.

Passionately fierce the voice of God is pleading,
   Pleading with men to arm them for the fight;
See how those hands, majestically bleeding,
   Call us to rout the armies of the night.

Not to the work of sordid selfish saving
   Of our own souls to dwell with Him on high,
But to the soldier's splendid selfless braving,
   Eager to fight for Righteousness and die.

Peace does not mean the end of all our striving,
   Joy does not mean the drying of our tears;
Peace is the power that comes to souls arriving
   Up to the light where God Himself appears.

Joy is the wine that God is ever pouring
   Into the hearts of those who strive with Him,
Light'ning their eyes to vision and adoring,
   Strength'ning their arms to warfare glad and grim.

So would I live and not in idle resting,
   Stupid as swine that wallow in the mire;
Fain would I fight, and be for ever breasting
   Danger and death for ever under fire.

Bread of Thy Body give me for my fighting,
   Give me to drink Thy Sacred Blood for wine,
While there are wrongs that need me for the righting,
   While there is warfare splendid and divine.

Give me, for light, the sunshine of Thy sorrow,
   Give me, for shelter, shadow of Thy Cross;
Give me to share the glory of Thy morrow,
   Gone from my heart the bitterness of Loss.

FAITH

How do I know that God is good?   I don't.
I gamble like a man.   I bet my life
Upon one side in life's great war.   I must,
I can't stand out.   I must take sides.   The man
Who is a neutral in this fight is not
A man.   He's bulk and body without breath,
Cold leg of lamb without mint sauce.   A fool.
He makes me sick.   Good Lord!   Weak tea!
    Cold slops!
I want to live, live out, not wobble through
My life somehow, and then into the dark.
I must have God.   This life's too dull without,
Too dull for aught but suicide.   What's man
To live for else?   I'd murder some one just
To see red blood.   I'd drink myself blind drunk,
And see blue snakes if I could not look up
To see blue skies, and hear God speaking through
The silence of the stars.   How is it proved?
It isn't proved, you fool, it can't be proved.
How can you prove a victory before
It's won?   How can you prove a man who leads,
To be a leader worth the following,

Unless you follow to the death—and out
Beyond mere death, which is not anything
But Satan's lie upon eternal life?
Well—God's my leader, and I hold that He
Is good, and strong enough to work His plan
And purpose out to its appointed end.
I am no fool, I have my reasons for
This faith, but they are not the reasonings,
The coldly calculated formulæ
Of thought divorced from feeling.   They are true,
Too true for that.   There's no such thing as thought
Which does not feel, if it be real thought
And not thought's ghost—all pale and sicklied o'er
With dead conventions—abstract truth—man's lie
Upon this living, loving, suff'ring Truth,
That pleads and pulses in my very veins,
The blue blood of all beauty, and the breath
Of life itself.   I see what God has done,
What life in this world is.   I see what you
See, this eternal struggle in the dark.
I see the foul disorders, and the filth
Of mind and soul, in which men, wallowing
Like swine, stamp on their brothers till they drown
In puddles of stale blood, and vomitings
Of their corruption.   This life stinks in places,
'Tis true, yet scent of roses and of hay
New mown comes stealing on the evening breeze,
And through the market's din, the bargaining
Of cheats, who make God's world a den of thieves,
I hear sweet bells ring out to prayer, and see
The faithful kneeling by the Calvary
Of Christ.

      I walk in crowded streets where men
And women, mad with lust, loose-lipped and lewd
Go promenading down to hell's wide gates;
Yet have I looked into my mother's eyes,

And seen the light that never was on sea
Or land, the light of Love, pure Love and true,
And on that Love I bet my life.   I back
My mother 'gainst a whore when I believe
In God, and can a man do less or more?
I have to choose.   I back the scent of life
Against its stink.   That's what Faith works out at
Finally.   I know not why the Evil,
I know not why the Good, both mysteries
Remain unsolved, and both insoluble.
I know that both are there, the battle set,
And I must fight on this side or on that.
I can't stand shiv'ring on the bank, I plunge
Head first.   I bet my life on Beauty, Truth,
And Love, not abstract but incarnate Truth,
Not Beauty's passing shadow but its Self.
Its very self made flesh, Love realised.
I bet my life on Christ—Christ Crucified.
Behold your God!   My soul cries out.   He hangs,
Serenely patient in His agony,
And turns the soul of darkness into light.
I look upon that body, writhing, pierced
And torn with nails, and see the battlefields
Of time, the mangled dead, the gaping wounds,
The sweating, dazed survivors straggling back,
The widows worn and haggard, still dry-eyed,
Because their weight of sorrow will not lift
And let them weep; I see the ravished maid,
The honest mother in her shame; I see
All history pass by, and through it all
Still shines that face, the Christ Face, like a star
Which pierces drifting clouds, and tells the Truth.
They pass, but it remains and shines untouched,
A pledge of that great hour which surely comes
When storm winds sob to silence, fury spent
To silver silence, and the moon sails calm

And stately through the soundless seas of Peace.
So through the clouds of Calvary—there shines
His face, and I believe that Evil dies,
And Good lives on, loves on, and conquers all—
All War must end in Peace.   These clouds are lies.
They cannot last.   The blue sky is the Truth.
For God is love.   Such is my Faith, and such
My reasons for it, and I find them strong
Enough.   And you?   You want to argue?   Well,
I can't.   It is a choice.   I choose the Christ.

IF JESUS NEVER LIVED

Suppose it is not true,
And Jesus never lived,
But only grew,
Like Aphrodite, from the foam
Of fancy—
From the sea
Of pure imagining, that frets
Within the soul eternally.
Suppose the Word was not made flesh,
But just another dream,
Which dwelt amongst us, only
As a gleam
Of glory from the land,
Where sand
Is gold, and golden sand
Shines bright beside the sapphire sea.
Where up is down,
And down is up,
And mortals mount on wings,
To sup
From golden goblets

With young stars
The nectar of eternity;
Where trees have souls,
And lilies arms
To fold us in,
And charms
To soothe our sorrows into peace.
Where cease,
And sink to silence
Of content,
The sad complainings
Man has sent
To heaven's high throne
All down the years,
Where bitter tears
Are turned to diamonds for the crown of God
Suppose He never trod
This earth nor saw the sun,
Nor looked up to the skies,
That sinless one,
All spotless clean,
Untainted by man's curse,
The might have been,
The ghost of good undone.
Suppose the gospel story lies,
What then?   Why, then
There are no fairies
Any more
For men,
The shore
Of fairyland is dry,
Unlapped by any sea.
All fancies die,
If Jesus never lived,
For living fancies need to be
The symbols of a Truth.

He is the door
By which we enter in
To wonderland.
By Christ's strong sooth
Set free from sin,
Poor Cinderella weds her Prince,
As we long since
Were taught and may believe,
For God is found of those who seek,
Exalts the humble and the meek,
And puts the mighty from their seats,
In Christ.
Her tryst,
If Jesus never lived,
Is still unkept;
By those dead ashes where she wept
For Paradise,
She weeps on still,
And moans upon her fate;
The pumpkins still are pumpkins,
And the mice still mice;
Still by the cold and empty grate
She sits in rags and tears;
Through all the years—the empty years,
No fairy comes—nor ever will
If Jesus never lived.
In Christ's pure light,
Fair Snowy-White
Can lift the coffin-lid,
And leave her tomb,
And vanquish all the gloom
Of death.
Because He lives
And gives
To Sleeping Beauty
One long kiss,

She opens her blue eyes and wakes,
Forsakes
Her sleep and shines for ever,
Beautiful in bliss.
There is no chance of childhood,
But for this
One Child of God, who knew
That childhood's sweetest dreams come true,
And was their Truth.
Lord Jesus, live for me,
Open my eyes to see
Thy face,
So by Thy Grace
Shall all the world be peopled
By bright forms.
The wind of many voices,
In its storms,
Shall speak of Giant powers,
The many-coloured flowers
Shall hold their lips up for a kiss.
Still in the deep
Shall mermaids sleep,
And dryads from the oak tree
Stretch white hands,
While through the leaves,
Small faces peep
And laugh in elfin revelry,
Binding with silken bands
My spirit to the glades.
So shall my soul swing free
Of this small world,
And dance with daffodilly maids,
Amid the bluebells in the sun.
O live for me, Thou sinless one,
Cleanse Thou for me
The earth and sea,

Sweep all the clouds from off
   The sky,
For fancies never, never die
   If only Jesus lives.

PATIENCE

Sometimes I wish that I might do
   Just one grand deed and die,
And by that one grand deed reach up
   To meet God in the sky.
But such is not Thy way, O God,
   Not such is Thy decree,
But deed by deed, and tear by tear,
   Our souls must climb to Thee,
As climbed the only Son of God
   From manger unto Cross,
Who learned, through tears and bloody sweat,
   To count this world but loss;
Who left the Virgin Mother's Arms
   To seek those arms of shame,
Outstretched upon the lonely hill
   To which the darkness came.
As deed by deed, and tear by tear,
   He climbed up to the height,
Each deed a splendid deed, each tear
   A jewel shining bright,
So grant us, Lord, the patient heart,
   To climb the upward way,
Until we stand upon the height,
   And see the perfect day.

HER GIFT

Dead black against a blood-red sky
      It stands,
With outstretched hands,
      The Calvary.
What can it mean,
Beyond the vain recalling of a scene,
A shameful scene of centuries ago?
And yet, if that be so,
      How can it be,
      For you and me,
A thing of any worth at all?
We've seen men die,
Not once, nor twice, but many times
      In agony
As ghastly to behold as that.
We've seen men fall,
And rise, and staggering onward fall again,
Bedrenched in their own blood,
Fast flowing like a flood,
Of crimson sacrifice upon the snow.
We've seen, and would forget.
Why then should there be set
Before our eyes these monuments of crime?
It's time, high time,
That they were buried in the past;
There let them lie,
In that great sea of merciful oblivion,
      Where our vile deeds,
      And outworn creeds,
      Are left to rot and die.
      We would forget,
      And yet,

Do you remember Rob McNeil
            And how he died,
            And cried,
And pleaded with his men
            To take that gun,
            And kill the Hun
            That worked it, dead?
            He bled
Horribly.   Do you remember?
I can't forget,
I would not if I could,
It were not right I should;
            He died for me.
He was a God, that boy,
The only God I could adore.
And that reminds me I have something here
He wore:
He gave it me that night,
But because my heart was sore
With grief, I have not dared to look at it.
But here it is, a little leather case,
A picture, maybe, of the face
That smiled upon him as a babe,
            All wondering bright,
            With mother light,
Of tenderest pride and love.
The face that oft would dimple into laughter
At his first baby tricks.
It is her gift: but look at it—
            A little silver Crucifix.

TEMPTATION

Pray! Have I prayed! When I'm worn with all my
  praying!
  When I've bored the blessed angels with my battery of
  prayer!
It's the proper thing to say — but it's only saying, saying,
  And I cannot get to Jesus for the glory of her hair.

IDOLS

Think ye the ancient Gods are dead?
  They live and work their will,
Before their shrines the sons of men
  Bow down and grovel still.

Still Venus stands with swelling breasts
  And sidelong glancing eyes,
And lures lust-drunken devotees,
  To trust her when she lies.

The ancient lie that lust is Love
  And passion what it seems,
A lotus land where men may find
  The heaven of their dreams.

The old eternal cruel smile
  That lulls men's souls to sleep,
And wraps them in a paradise
  That they may wake — and weep.

She smiles and counts her victims up—
    Young wife and little child,
The festering filth of bodies
    By lures of lust defiled.

Blind babies crying for the light,
    Strong men with open sores,
The never-ceasing sacrifice
    Streams through her temple doors.

And last of all, her captive King,
    With bleeding hands and feet,
Still burdened with the crushing Cross,
    Christ comes—and passing sweet

To her lascivious, mocking eyes
    The sight of Him must be,
The brightest jewel in her crown
    Christ's bitter agony.

She still can take and lead Him bound
    To some poor altar place,
Where weary disappointed souls
    Creep in to see His face.

And laughing loud can leave Him there,
    To nurse His wounded feet,
While she fares forth in flaming robes,
    To sway the surging street.

There mid the dust of dying creeds
    Christ starves, while Venus feasts;
She holds the people's hearts, and leaves
    To Him—the mumbling priests.

THE TRUTH OF MAY

Dear land of May,
The wise men say,
That there is naught behind
Thee but a force,
A million forces,
Purposeless and blind,
That wind and wind
In wandering courses,
Unto no end
But nothingness at last.
No Father, Friend
Of Man has made thee,
But a chance,
A sudden chance,
That happened blindly in the dance
Of Atoms that is past,
They say.
Well, let them say,
These bearded grey
Blind fools with spectacles,
And goggling eyes,
Glued to their books,
That seek the living mid the dead,
The dust of theories they have read,
And weave great lies
To cheat child souls of May.
They make me laugh,
Great solemn owls,
That sit up blinking in the night,
And prove that light
Is darkness, and the sun a moon,
Because it is too bright

For their dull souls to see,
The mystery
Of May is not revealed
To such as these,
'Tis signed and sealed;
The talk of trees,
The music of the meadows,
The wizardry
Of this small stream,
That sings—and sings—and dances,
While sudden sunlight glances,
In a silvery gleam,
Through fresh green leaves,
That overhang the bank,
And weaves
A diamond necklace for that mossy rock.
These only mock
The learned with their rude, rank
Truths of science and their books.
The poetry of brooks
Is deeper than their prose,
Owls—let them reason and welcome,
Here is a heart that knows
The truth of May,
And walks the way,
By which its fairy beauty leads,
Through woods and lanes,
With haunting strains
Of magic music, sowing seeds
Of summer in the sod,
Until she finds her fulness,
And bows down in adoration
'Mid the yellow cowslips
At the golden feet of God.

THE COMRADE GOD

Thou who dost dwell in depths of timeless being,
  Watching the years as moments passing by,
Seeing the things that lie beyond our seeing,
  Constant, unchanged, as æons dawn and die;

Thou who canst count the stars upon their courses,
  Holding them all in the hollow of Thy hand,
Lord of the world with its myriad of forces
  Seeing the hills as single grains of sand;

Art Thou so great that this our bitter crying
  Sounds in Thine ears like sorrow of a child?
Hast Thou looked down on centuries of sighing,
  And, like a heartless mother, only smiled?
Since in Thy sight to-day is as to-morrow,
  And while we strive Thy victory is won,
Hast Thou no tears to shed upon our sorrow?
  Art Thou a staring splendour like the sun?

Dost Thou not heed the helpless sparrow's falling?
  Canst Thou not see the tears that women weep?
Canst Thou not hear Thy little children calling?
  Dost Thou not watch above them as they sleep?

Then, O my God, Thou art too great to love me,
  Since Thou dost reign beyond the reach of tears,
Calm and serene as the cruel stars above me,
  High and remote from human hopes and fears.

Only in Him can I find home to hide me,
  Who on the Cross was slain to rise again;
Only with Him, my Comrade God, beside me,
  Can I go forth to war with sin and pain.

WASTE

Waste of Muscle, waste of Brain,
Waste of Patience, waste of Pain,
Waste of Manhood, waste of Health,
Waste of Beauty, waste of Wealth,
Waste of Blood, and waste of Tears,
Waste of Youth's most precious years,
Waste of ways the Saints have trod,
Waste of Glory, waste of God, —
          War!

YOUTH

Love's life and death,
God sets them both before me now.
And I perforce must choose.
Death seems so safe,
And Life so full of danger,
An adventure wild,
Wherein I stand to gain or lose
          So much.
Life and Love,
She stands for both, the Child,
With her bright eyes and sun-tanned face,
And when she turns to smile at me,
I have no place
          For fear;
The venture calls me, and I follow in my heart,
I long to launch my boat
          Upon forbidden seas,
And float

For years toward the sunrise
Where the trees
At even shelter lovers of a swarthier race,
Whose blood runs fire through their veins,
And Love bestows more freely
          Fiercer pleasures, fiercer pains.
Ah Love, is 't true
That thou art ofttimes cruel to the Loved?
Is there no certain refuge in thine arms,
And will the charms
Of thy soft beauty
          Fade away?
Is it only duty
          That is strong?
His visage is so marred,
His face so pale,
And round him ever I can hear the wail
Of those who lived in pain
And died in agony.
O Love, must I leave thee for this,
Forsake thine arms to gain one ice-cold kiss
From those pale lips?
Why is God's Love so cold?
Why does it seem so pale and old
Compared with hers,
Compared with hers which pleads and pulses in my blood,
Or sweeps across my senses like a flood
Of golden joy?

It is not fair, this choice,
God's Love is just a voice,
A still small voice that whispers and is gone.
So small this voice,
Yet it persists,
And by persistence pierces passion through with pain,
And twists

30

What once was triumph into torture of the soul.
My God, is there no whole
Where Peace and Passion meet
        And are at rest?

INDIFFERENCE

When Jesus came to Golgotha they hanged Him on a tree,
They drave great nails through hands and feet, and made a
    Calvary;
They crowned Him with a crown of thorns, red were His
    wounds and deep,
For those were crude and cruel days, and human flesh was
    cheap.

When Jesus came to Birmingham they simply passed Him
    by,
They never hurt a hair of Him, they only let Him die;
For men had grown more tender, and they would not give
    Him pain,
They only just passed down the street, and left Him in the
    rain.

Still Jesus cried, "Forgive them, for they know not what
    they do,"
And still it rained the wintry rain that drenched Him through
    and through;
The crowds went home and left the streets without a soul to
    see,
And Jesus crouched against a wall and cried for Calvary.

A SERMON

My brethren, the ways of God
   No man can understand,
We can but wait in awe and watch
   The wonders of His hand.
He dwells in Majesty sublime
   Beyond the starry height,
His Wisdom is ineffable,
   His Love is infinite.
Before Him all created things
   Do bow them and obey,
The million stars that night by night
   Wheel down the Milky Way.
The shrieking storm obeys His Will,
   The wild waves hear His call,
The mountain and the midge's wing,
   God made and governs all.
'Tis not for us to question Him,
   To ask or reason why,
'Tis ours to love and worship Him,
   And serve Him till we die.
O weeping Mother torn with grief,
   Poor stricken heart that cries,
And rocks a cradle empty now,
   'Tis by God's will he dies.
His strong young body blown to bits,
   His raw flesh quiv'ring still,
His comrades' groans of agony,
   These are God's Holy Will.
He measures out our Peace and War
   As seemeth to Him best,
His judgments are unknowable,
   Remember that—and rest.

For what are we poor worms of earth,
    Whose life is for a day,
Our finite minds that Satan blinds,
    My brethren, what are they?
We are but little children weak
    Who cling to God's right hand;
Just think how wonderful He is,
    And bow to His command.
He has some hidden purpose sure
    For all this blood and tears,
It is His Will—be still—be still,
    He is the Lord of years.
He bids us love our enemies,
    And live in Christian Peace,
'Tis only He can order Wars
    And woes that never cease.
Vengeance is Mine, I will repay;
    Beware! Thou shalt not kill:
Behold the bloody fields of France,
    They are God's Holy Will.
That is what makes Him wonderful
    To our poor human sight;
He only can work miracles
    And turn Wrong into Right.
So bow you down and worship Him,
    Kneel humbly and adore
This Infinitely Loving God
    Who is the Lord of War.
Lift up your hands in ceaseless prayer
    That He will spare your lives,
And let His loving judgments fall
    On other people's wives.
He is a God who answers prayer,
    And alters His decrees,
If only we persistently
    Beseech Him on our knees.

If only we would pray enough,
  My brethren, for our sons,
Then He would save their lives for us,
  And spike the German guns.
Our shrieks of pain go up in vain,
  The wide world's miseries
Must still persist until we learn
  To pray upon our knees.
Upon our knees, my friends, I said,
  And mark well what I say,
God wants to see us on our knees,
  The proper place to pray.
Nought is impossible to God
  In answer to such prayers;
If only we are meek enough,
  He is a God who spares.
Whenever people seek to know
  And ask the reason why
Their sons are swallowed up by wars,
  And called to fight and die,
There is one thing I ask, dear friends,
  One thing I always say,
I ask them straight, I'm not afraid,
  I ask them, "Did you pray?
Did you pray humbly on your knees
  That it might be God's Will
To spare his life and bring him back,
  To spare, and not to kill?"
Then if they still can answer Yes,
  And think to baffle me,
I simply answer, "Bow your head,
  His death was God's decree."
And who are we to question it,
  Who crawl upon the earth
As insects in His holy sight,
  Vile things of little worth?

Remember, rather, all your sins,
   And bow to God's decrees.
Seek not to know the plans of God,
   But pray upon your knees
That you may love with all your heart,
   With all your soul and mind,
This perfect God you cannot know,
   Whose face you cannot find.
You have no notion what He's like,
   You cannot know His Will,
He's wrapped in darkest mystery,
   But you must love Him still,
And love Him all the more because
   He is the unknown God
Who leads you blindfold down the path
   That martyred Saints have trod.
That is the Gospel of the Christ,
   Submit whate'er betides;
You cannot make the wrong world right,
   'Tis God alone decides.

.   .   .   .   .

O, by Thy Cross and Passion, Lord,
   By broken hearts that pant
For comfort and for love of Thee,
   Deliver us from cant.

A MOTHER UNDERSTANDS

Dear Lord, I hold my hand to take
   Thy Body, broken here for me,
Accept the Sacrifice I make,
   My body, broken, there, for Thee.

His was my body, born of me,
　　Born of my bitter travail pain,
And it lies broken on the field,
　　Swept by the wind and the rain.

Surely a Mother understands Thy thorn-crowned head,
The mystery of Thy piercèd hands — the Broken Bread.

SOLOMON IN ALL HIS GLORY

Still I see them coming, coming
　　In their ragged broken line,
Walking wounded in the sunlight,
　　Clothed in majesty divine.

For the fairest of the lilies,
　　That God's summer ever sees,
Ne'er was clothed in royal beauty
　　Such as decks the least of these.

Tattered, torn, and bloody khaki,
　　Gleams of white flesh in the sun,
Raiment worthy of their beauty
　　And the great things they have done.

Purple robes and snowy linen
　　Have for earthly kings sufficed,
But these bloody sweaty tatters
　　Were the robes of Jesus Christ.

HIS MATE

There's a broken, battered village
   Somewhere up behind the line,
There's a dug-out and a bunk there
   That I used to say were mine.

I remember how I reached them,
   Dripping wet and all forlorn,
In the dim and dreary twilight
   Of a weeping summer morn.

All that week I'd buried brothers,
   In one bitter battle slain,
In one grave I laid two hundred.
   God! What sorrow and what rain!

And that night I'd been in trenches,
   Seeking out the sodden dead,
And just dropping them in shell-holes,
   With a service swiftly said.

For the bullets rattled round me,
   But I couldn't leave them there,
Water-soaked in flooded shell-holes,
   Reft of common Christian prayer.

So I crawled round on my belly,
   And I listened to the roar
Of the guns that hammered Thiepval,
   Like big breakers on the shore.

Then there spoke a dripping sergeant,
   When the time was growing late,
"Would you please to bury this one,
   'Cause 'e used to be my mate?"

So we groped our way in darkness
    To a body lying there,
Just a blacker lump of blackness,
    With a red blotch on his hair.

Though we turned him gently over,
    Yet I still can hear the thud,
As the body fell face forward,
    And then settled in the mud.

We went down upon our faces,
    And I said the service through,
From "I am the Resurrection"
    To the last, the great "adieu."

We stood up to give the Blessing,
    And commend him to the Lord,
When a sudden light shot soaring
    Silver swift and like a sword.

At a stroke it slew the darkness,
    Flashed its glory on the mud,
And I saw the sergeant staring
    At a crimson clot of blood.

There are many kinds of sorrow
    In this world of Love and Hate,
But there is no sterner sorrow
    Than a soldier's for his mate.

AT A SÉANCE

"Is this so well-known voice
    That speaks

38

Just as he used to do of yore,
     With just that turning of the words—
Is it some trick of my subconscious self
     And nothing more,
Or is it truth,
     That from some other world
My love is knocking at the door?

"I could have sworn it was his voice
     That spoke, it woke
So many sweet responsive echoes
     In my soul,
And stole across my senses
     As his voice was wont to do
In thrills of golden joy.

"And yet, and yet
     It may be that I can't forget
Because he lives in me,
     And through and through
My soul is drenched with his,
     And memory
Plays some wild jest.

"Dear God, wouldst Thou permit
     So vile a lie
To trick a poor forsaken heart,
     And break the rest,
     The troubled rest,
That time allows me from my grief?

"But why should this be viler
     Than the million lies
That lure men to destruction every day?
     So many stars are lit

Up in the sky
   That lead men nowhere
But to some grey
   Dawn of sorrow and a barren shore,
Where naught remains of their dead dream
   But an exceeding bitter cry,
And that cry's echo, 'Nevermore.'"

HIGH AND LIFTED UP

Seated on the throne of power with the sceptre in Thine
   hand,
While a host of eager angels ready for Thy Service stand.
So it was the prophet saw Thee, in his agony of prayer,
While the sound of many waters swelled in music on the
   air,
Swelled until it burst like thunder in a shout of perfect
   praise,
"Holy, Holy, Holy Father, Potentate of years and days.
Thine the Kingdom, Thine the glory, Thine the splendour
   of the sun,
Thine the wisdom, Thine the honour, Thine the crown of
   victory won."
So it was the prophet saw Thee, so this artist saw Thee
   too,
Flung his vision into colour, mystery of gold and blue.
But I stand in woe and wonder; God, my God, I cannot
   see,
Darkness deep and deeper darkness—all the world is dark
   to me.
Where is power? Where is glory? Where is any victory
   won?
Where is wisdom? Where is honour? Where the splendour of the sun?

God, I hate this splendid vision—all its splendour is a lie,
Splendid fools see splendid folly, splendid mirage born to
die.
As imaginary waters to an agony of thirst,
As the vision of a banquet to a body hunger-cursed,
As the thought of anæsthetic to a soldier mad with pain,
While his torn and tortured body turns and twists and
writhes again,
So this splendid lying vision turns within my doubting
heart,
Like a bit of rusty bayonet in a torn and festering part.
Preachers give it me for comfort, and I curse them to their
face,
Puny, petty-minded priestlings prate to me of power and
grace;
Prate of power and boundless wisdom that takes count of
little birds,
Sentimental poisoned sugar in a sickening stream of words.
Platitudinously pious far beyond all doubts and fears,
They will patter of God's mercy that can wipe away our
tears.
All their speech is drowned in sobbing, and I hear the great
world groan,
As I see a million mothers sitting weeping all alone,
See a host of English maidens making pictures in the fire,
While a host of broken bodies quiver still on German wire.
And I hate the God of Power on His hellish heavenly
throne,
Looking down on rape and murder, hearing little children
moan.
Though a million angels hail Thee King of Kings, yet can-
not I.
There is nought can break the silence of my sorrow save
the cry,
"Thou who rul'st this world of sinners with Thy heavy
iron rod,

Was there ever any sinner who has sinned the sin of God?
Was there ever any dastard who would stand and watch
a Hun
Ram his bayonet through the bowels of a baby just for fun?
Praise to God in Heaven's highest and in all the depths be
praise,
Who in all His works is brutal, like a beast in all His
ways."
God, the God I love and worship, reigns in sorrow on the
Tree,
Broken, bleeding, but unconquered, very God of God
to me.
All that showy pomp of splendour, all that sheen of angel
wings,
Was but borrowed from the baubles that surround our
earthly kings.
Thought is weak and speech is weaker, and the vision
that He sees
Strikes with dumbness any preacher, brings him humbly to
his knees.
But the word that Thou hast spoken borrows nought from
kings and thrones,
Vain to rack a royal palace for the echo of Thy tones.
In a manger, in a cottage, in an honest workman's shed,
In the homes of humble peasants, and the simple lives
they led,
In the life of one an outcast and a vagabond on earth,
In the common things He valued, and proclaimed of price-
less worth,
And above all in the horror of the cruel death He died,
Thou hast bid us seek Thy glory, in a criminal crucified.
And we find it—for Thy glory is the glory of Love's loss,
And Thou hast no other splendour but the splendour of
the Cross.
For in Christ I see the martyrs and the beauty of their
pain,

And in Him I hear the promise that my dead shall rise
    again.
High and lifted up, I see Him on the eternal Calvary,
And two piercèd hands are stretching east and west o'er
    land and sea.
On my knees I fall and worship that great Cross that shines
    above,
For the very God of Heaven is not Power, but Power of
    Love.

SET YOUR AFFECTIONS ON THINGS ABOVE

How far above the things of earth
    Is Christ at God's right hand?
How far above yon snowy peaks
    Do His white angels stand?

Must we fare forth to seek a world
    Beyond that silent star?
Forsake these dear familiar homes
    And climb the heights—How far?

As far as meaning is from speech,
    As beauty from a rose,
As far as music is from sound,
    As poetry from prose,

As far as art from cleverness,
    As painting is from paints,
As far as signs from sacraments,
    As Pharisees from Saints,

As far as love from friendship is,
  As reason is from Truth,
As far as laughter is from joy,
  And early years from youth,

As far as love from shining eyes,
  As passion from a kiss,
So far is God from God's green earth,
  So far that world from this.

ONLY ENGAGED

I can hear their voices singing as the train steams slowly
    out,
  I can see their faces still through mists of tears;
I can see brown hands still waving as I wrench my soul
    about,
  To the weary days that lengthen into years.

I can see two eyes that soften as they seek to fathom mine,
  I can see two strong lips trembling to a smile,
I can see a dear face lighten with a human love divine,
  And sweet mem'ries bear my burden for a while.

Then a downy head comes seeking for the pillow of my
    breast,
  And a gleeful voice calls chuckling for its Dad,
And with two small arms around it my soul sinks back to
    rest,
  Singing nonsense to the child we never had.

WILD ROSE WAY

My dear, I love you as I love
Wild roses when they first come out
In June, with that miraculous
Soft blush of pink, as though some elf
Had painted them for fun, while God
Looked on and laughed.   You know the way
They nod and ask you not to pluck
Them, please, because they fade so soon.
I never want to touch, but just
To stand, and stare, and stare, and thank
The God who made them, and gave me
Eyes to see.   That's how I love you,
Dear, wild rose way.   It is pure joy
To look on you, June morning joy,
But oh! how I hate death, dull death,
When I see roses or see you.
For you ought not to die, or change,
Or grow, or bloom, or fade, wild rose,
You should be always you, the same
Eternal summer, with the dew
For ever fresh upon your hair.
And I should never die, or age,
I hate this growing old that blinds
Our eyes, and steals sweet laughter from
Our hearts.   It should be always June.
And we should just stand still and stare,
Until we see pure Beauty's face,
And kiss the garment hem of God.

NON ANGLI SED ANGELI

"Not Angles merely but of angel stock,
These boys blue-eyed and shining from the sea,
Which like a silver girdle belts their home.
Not slaves, but souls, not tools to use for gain,
But men to love and lead and save for God
Who made them; and for that great King who died
The death of shame and glory on the Cross."
So spake the master Christian of the world
Long years ago when, in the streets of Rome
Imperial, he met the ancestors
Of that yet greater Rome which was to be.
So spake he, taught by Him to whose great soul
There were no slaves nor chattels in the world
But only men and brothers, Sons of God,
The last and greatest works of wondrous Love,
From whose eternal energy of pain
The greatest and the least of things is sprung.
So spake he, taught by Him who mirrored forth
To men's blind eyes that Love divine of God,
Who, like a father, mourns the one lost son,
And, like a faithful shepherd, wanders wide
Across the hills and calls through dawnless dark
The one lost sheep that strays forth from the fold.
Christ lived in him, and he had learned full well
The first and chiefest lesson of His life,
The value of a man to God, the price
God puts on human souls, the price of blood
And pain paid out in coin of Calvary.
And in that blazing light of Love he saw
The sin of slavery, the sin supreme,
That slays the world because it values life
As death, and dares to use as mere machines,

For pleasure or for profit, living men.
This blasphemy against the Holy Ghost,
Which, neither in this world nor in the next,
Can find forgiveness in the heart of God,
Who only knows the value of a man,
He saw it with the eyes of Christ, and spoke
In all unconscious prophecy, the doom
Of slavery, which these same blue-eyed boys
Would one day die to banish from the world.
And I have seen them die in these last days:
Yes, I have seen their bright blue eyes grow dim
With agony, yet never lose their smile,
The dauntless smile of Angles that reveals
Their angel souls, and crowns them Kings by right,
The destined saviours of the world from sin,
And from the curse of tyranny which kills
The souls of men, and turns them into slaves.
Yes, I have seen them smile at death, and known,
By instinct of sure prophecy, the Truth
That seas of dead tyrannic force would break
In vain against the rock of British hearts,
Whereon the love of freedom sits enthroned.
This have I known, and have with tears rejoiced,
Until there shivered through me like the chill
Of death, the fear lest gold be strong where steel
Is weak; lest men whose pride no sword can slay
May yet be bought and sold to slavery.
The day of tyrant kings is dead, and thrones
Shall nevermore dethrone men's souls.   But now
A dull inhuman monster takes their place.
The minotaur of Mammon tears the wings
From new-fledged souls and flings them bleeding down
To dogs of greed and lust.   To him they are
Dead hands, machines that make machines, and grind
Out gold to swell the coffers of the rich.
They have no right to fly, their wings are best

Cut short, that so their hands may be more strong
To work, make wealth, build up the State, and set
The Commonwealth on sure foundations, made
Of gold and silver and of precious stones.
To him a man is of less value than
A beast of burden, for the beast must needs
Be bought for gold, and if he dies be bought
Again, but men need not be bought; they are
Machines for hire that can be scrapped at will,
And new ones hired with no fresh cost at all,
Because they die or weaken in their work.
Supply is plentiful, and men are drugs
Upon the crowded markets of the world.
So Satan takes new forms, and when he finds
The sword is weak, too weak to win brave hearts
As slaves, creeps snakelike in, in time of Peace,
To fetter free-born men with golden chains
And lead them helpless captives down to hell.
O England, when this wave of war is spent,
And rolls back baffled from thy rocky breast,
Wilt thou be strong to slay the Minotaur,
And strangle that great golden snake that crept
In time of Peace about thy home to kill,
With venom of low greed and lust of wealth,
The soul of Freedom and the heart of Love?
Shall wealth still grow, and woe increase to breed
In filthy slums the slaves of poverty?
Shall senseless pride and vulgar luxury
By gilding over evil make it good?
Shall souls be only hands again, dead hands,
That toil for wealth that makes none rich save those
Who need it not? Shall men still seek in drink
A refuge from the burden of their strife,
And from that dull monotony of grey
That shadows half our cities from the sun?
Shall women still be bought and sold, like dogs

Upon the streets, because the wage they earn
By work will not keep bodies for their souls?
Shall children come to birth, too weak to live,
Not even hands of strength, but feeble hands,
That clutch at life and die—just born to die
And cry—cry shame upon the grimy world
That murdered them? If this be what must come,
Then blessed are the dead who die in war,
Their bodies shattered, but their souls untouched
By slime of sin, unpoisoned by the snake,
For war is kinder than a Godless peace.
O England, let this message from the past
Ring down the ages like a trumpet call,
Not Angles these but Angels, souls not slaves,
Let not thy wealth be counted in base coin
But in chaste mothers, comely maids, strong men
With kindly eyes, in sound of children's play,
And in those happy aged ones who stand
Between the seas of life, and, looking back
And forwards, vow that human life is good.
So must our land be reckoned rich or poor.

DEATH

If death be just a last long sleep,
   Then death were good, men say;
Yet say it knowing naught of sleep
   Save light at dawn of day.

For sleep's a blank—a nothingness,
   A thing we cannot know;
We can but taste the streams of life
   That from its fountain flow.

When day puts off her gorgeous robes,
   And darkness veils our sight,
Lest we should see her beauty laid
   Upon the couch of night,

We crave for sleep because we hold
   A memory of morn,
The rush of life renewed, that with
   The birth of day is born.

So weary souls that crave for death,
   As sweet and dreamless sleep,
As night when men may cease to war,
   And women cease to weep,

Are longing still for life—more life,
   Their souls not yet sufficed,
Cry out for God's eternal streams;
   They crave not death—but Christ.

TREES

Once glistering green,
With dewy sheen,
And summer glory round them cast:
Now black and bare,
The trees stand there,
And mourn their beauty that is past.

Look, leaf by leaf,
Each leaf a grief,
The hand of Autumn strips them bare.
No sound nor cry,
As they fall and die,
Because they know that Life is there.

So stiff and strong,
The winter long,
All uncomplaining stand the trees.
God make my life,
Through all its strife,
As true to Spring as one of these.

So would I stand,
Serene and grand,
While age strips off the joys of youth;
Because I know
That, as they go,
My soul draws nearer to the Truth.

He is the Truth,
In very sooth,
The Word made flesh, who dwelt with men,
And the world shall ring
With the song of Spring,
When thy soul turns to its Lord again.

When God's soft breath,
That men call death,
Falls gently on thy closing eyes,
Thy youth, that goes
Like the red June rose,
Shall burst to bloom in Paradise.

AT THE EUCHARIST

How through this Sacrament of simple things
The great God burns His way,
I know not— He is there.
The silent air

Is pulsing with the presence of His grace,
Almost I feel a face
Bend o'er me as I kneel,
While on my ears there steal
The strains of "Agnus Dei" softly sung.
How it calls—calls Heaven to earth,
Calls Christ to birth,
And pleads for man's Redemption
With his God.
Here star and sod
Unite to sing their Maker's praise,
While, through the windows, broken rays
Of crimson sunlight make a path
For Him to tread.
Just common bread?
The artist's colour blazing bright,
The subtle scheme of shade and light,
That thrills our souls to ecstasy,
Is bread.
The notes that wed,
And weave a wonderland of sound,
Wherein our hearts may wander round,
And reach the heart of God's red rose,
Where beauty dwells alone and grows
Sublime in solitude,
All these are bread.
Are they not born of earth and rain
Becoming tissue of man's brain,
The vehicle of every thought?
The Spirit that our God bestows,
The mystery that loves and knows,
The very soul our Saviour bought
Speaks through a body born of bread—
And wine.
The clinging vine
That climbs some crumbled wall in France,

Drinks in the Love of God,
His precious Blood,
Poured out in beams that dance
Through long-drawn summer days,
Swift golden rays of sunshine,
That are stored within the grape
Until it swells
And spills their splendour
Into wine
To fill the chalice of the Lord.
Then earth and heaven intertwine;
The Word
Takes flesh and dwells with men,
And once again
Dim eyes may see
His gentle glory shine,
The glory of humility,
Which in creation stoops .o raise,
Through time's eternity of days,
Our weakness to His strength,
For neither length,
Nor breadth nor depth nor height,
Stays now the piercing of that light
Of omnipresent Love,
It runs red fire through our veins;
The Life divine,
In common wine,
Thrills through the matter of our brains,
Begetting dreams,
And gleams
Of God—swift golden speech,
And charity that burns to reach
The very depths of hell,
And lift them up to Christ,
Who has our thirsty souls sufficed,
Till they are drunk with God.

JUDGMENT

There is mercy with Thee, therefore shalt Thou be feared.

I saw no thronged angelic court, I saw no great white
    throne,
I saw no open Judgment books, I seemed to stand alone.
I seemed to stand alone beside a solemn sounding sea,
While, at my feet upon the shore, broke waves of memory.
Their murmuring music sobbed and sought a way into my
    soul,
The perfect past was present there, and I could see it whole,
Its beauty and its ugliness, its sorrow and its sin,
Its splendour and its sordidness, as wave on wave rolled
    in.
And ever deeper pierced the pain of all that I had lost,
My dear dead dreams of perfect things, I saw them tempest-
    tossed.
They fell like wreckage at my feet, and, as I turned them
    o'er,
The solemn waves, in Memory's caves, kept booming
    "Never more!"
There came one dream, more dear than all, a corpse without
    a head,
The flying spray hissed cowardice, and it was dead, cold
    dead.
Then suddenly a shadow fell, and I was not alone,
He stood with me beside the sea, and listened to its
    moan.
I did not dare to raise my eyes, I feared what I might
    see,
A cold sweat broke and bathed my brow, I longed to turn
    and flee,
But could not; rooted there I stood, in shiv'ring shame
    and fear,

The subtle shadow substance took, and nearer came,
    and near.
O was it days or was it years, we stood beside that sea,
Or was it æons, timeless times? It seemed eternity.
At last, compelled, I raised my eyes. Two eyes looked
    into mine,
And shattered all my soul with shame, so sad and so
    divine.
It palsied all my pride with pain, the terror of those tears,
And wrought into my soul the woe of all my wasted years.
"Depart from me," I cried, "depart, I cannot stand with
    Thee
And face the sorrow of those eyes, beside this cruel
    sea.
Depart from me, I dare not tread the sands those feet have
    trod,
Nor look into those eyes that tell the agony of God.
Depart," I cried, and He was gone. I stood there all
    alone,
In silence save that Memory's sea still made perpetual
    moan.
Night shadowed all, and wandering winds came wailing
    from afar,
But out across the darkening sea shone forth one single
    star.

MY PEACE I GIVE UNTO
YOU

Blessed are the eyes that see
    The things that you have seen,
Blessed are the feet that walk
    The ways where you have been.

Blessed are the eyes that see
    The Agony of God,
Blessed are the feet that tread
    The paths His feet have trod.

Blessed are the souls that solve
    The paradox of Pain,
And find the path that, piercing it,
    Leads through to Peace again.

EASTER

There was rapture of spring in the morning
    When we told our love in the wood,
For you were the spring in my heart, dear lad,
    And I vowed that my life was good.

But there's winter of war in the evening,
    And lowering clouds overhead,
There's wailing of wind in the chimney nook,
    And I vow that my life lies dead.

For the sun may shine on the meadow lands,
    And the dog-rose bloom in the lanes,
But I've only weeds in my garden, lad,
    Wild weeds that are rank with the rains.

One solace there is for me, sweet but faint,
    As it floats on the wind of the years,
A whisper that spring is the last true thing,
    And that triumph is born of tears.

It comes from a garden of other days,
  And an echoing voice that cries,
"Behold I am alive for evermore,
  And in Me shall the dead arise."

RIGHT IS MIGHT

Ah yes, I know full well, this is,
It has to be, the end of things.
But would to God it were not so,
And we could live eternally,
As we lived that one last moment,
When you lay within my arms.
I never lived before, dear heart.
But that, alas! can never be,
It must be just a golden flash,
Like blooms that for a day adorn
The many-splendoured garb of God.
Then fading, fall to rot and die,
Returning, like poor ravished maids,
To Mother Earth, so coldly kind.
So must this moment of our lives,
Wherein their meaning has found bloom,
Be swallowed in that waste of years,
In which we do not live, but drift,
Drift outward with the tide of time,
To that dark l nd which no man knows.
It must be so.   But why, dear, why?
Why should we not make permanent
That paradisic moment of the past?
One movement, just a sign from you,
And once again our paradise
Would fold us both in such embrace

Of purest bliss, that conscience care
Could not pierce through to wound and maim.
Why then should we stand thus, ashamed,
With frightened eyes, like children caught
In some too sweet forbidden play?
Come, child, be brave, and take what's yours
For less than asking.   Raise your eyes,
One glance from them and heaven's ours.
What, downcast still?   A miracle.
What is there stands 'twixt you and me?
What can there be so strong that it
Avails to keep those eyes downcast,
Wherein I saw, a moment back,
The lamps of love gleam passionate?
"'Tis God," you say.   Then cursed be God
Who blights the beauty that I saw,
As though in this drab dreary world
Such beauty were a common thing,
And human souls were not half-starved
And stunted by the lack of that
Which gleamed in glory from your eyes.
Curse God who makes the lily die,
And rapes its beauty from the rose,
Who bids the sunset flame and fade,
And overburdens life with death.
Who gives our hearts enough to make
Us long for more, then takes away
The little that we have.   Who turns
Our sweetest passions into pains,
And will not give us even Peace,
Not even Peace in death, for we
Are tortured by our dream that death
Is dawn of immortality.
These endless ever-ending joys,
Whose aching beauty contradicts
The desperate hope of death they teach,

Still lure us on into the mist,
Where Truth abides.   If Truth there be.
I know.   'Tis madness.   Wind and words.
A clod defies its God.   Poor fool!
I do but hurl myself, my soul,
In futile fury 'gainst a wall
Immovable, not built with hands.
There must be Truth, since you are True.
This beauty dies at birth because
It is not Right.   O Power of Right,
That Thou should'st meet and conquer might
Is but a little thing; thy strength
Is only fully shown when Thou
Dost meet and conquer Love like mine.
Farewell, sweet soul of mine, farewell.

MAN'S SOUL

The Great God stooped to save my soul
    And lift it up to Paradise;
But something bound it still to earth,
    A careless woman's eyes.

Then Satan came to damn my soul,
    And drag it down to his own place;
But something bound it still to earth.
    Another woman's face.

A SONG OF THE DESERT

On the Hindenburg Line, 1918

I've sung my songs of battlefields,
   Of sacrifice and pain,
When all my soul was fain to sing
   Of sunshine and of rain.

Of dewdrops glist'ning on a rose,
   Cloud castles in blue skies,
Of glory as God's summer grows,
   And splendour as it dies.

Of blossom snowed upon the trees,
   And fresh green woods that ring
With music of the mating birds,
   Love's miracle of spring.

Of summer night in velvet robes,
   Bedecked with silver stars,
The captive beauty of the dawn
   That breaks her prison bars.

The rustling sigh of fallen leaves
   That sing beneath my feet
The swan-song of the autumn days,
   So short, so sad, so sweet.

An exile in a weary land,
   My soul sighs for release,
It wanders in war's wilderness,
   And cries for Peace—for Peace.

COME UNTO ME

A Shell-hole Meditation

Come unto Me, He said,
And I will give you rest.
Dear Lord, is that the best
That Thou canst give
To those who follow Thee,
To stand and see
The strife,
The everlasting war of Life,
Pass by as in a picture or a dream?
It is not thus I deem
Life should be lived;
It is not that I crave,
Not Rest, but strength to save
The wounded and console their pain,
To strive with evil and then strive again,
Until the far-off victory is won.
Not rest from life,
But strength for strife,
A strife unending till its task is done.
      That is my quest,
        Dear Lord, not Rest.
Not rest but strength,
Thy strength, O God, I seek,
For I am weak,
My spirit's weak,
My flesh is weaker still,
My body plays the traitor to my will,
And fails me at my need,
As though some fate decreed
That I should never be
The man I long to be,

Or see
The very vision that I seek.
And when my spirit's fain to fill
The measure of my manhood, still
I fail,
And, like the Holy Grail,
The Vision shines on yet ahead
And calls me on;
And I must tread
Where it has led,
However rough the road may be.
There may be rest for Thee,
My God, but not for me.
For I must fight:
It is not right
That I should cease,
And rest in Peace,
      A Peace my soul has never won.
My task can ne'er be done
Till I have found perfection at the least:
'Tis Thou hast made me so,
'Tis Thou must surely know
The sources of the strength I crave
To seek, to help, to save
The wandering and restore the lost,
Bring back to shore the tempest-tossed
And set their hungry bodies down to feast.
Give me, O Lord, a soldier's rest;
Who lies uneasy on the crest
Of some bare shell-swept hill,
And with the earth for pillow waits until
The dawn of battle breaks,
Then for his country's and his children's sakes
Goes forth to death,
While all around him heaves and quakes
The torn and battered earth,

And battle belches poison breath,
For in his soul finds birth
The Better Rest,
Which comes of Trust in one who leads,
Great joy in gallant knightly deeds,
And Love of that great cause for which he fights.
Oh, I have seen such sights
As make me long to know
The secret of that Rest
Which gives men strength
To suffer and endure the length
Of endless misery that war entails;
      For that were best,
To take that strength
And use it not to slay but sow
The seed of better worlds to be;
To use it, not to kill,
But rather fill
Men full of finer life,
  The life that never fails
To open their blind eyes
And make them see
The Vision of the Highest as He is,
     To seek and find the better way
     By which men go forth not to slay
But save men from their miseries.
     O God, is hate more strong than Love,
     And is the life that's born above
So weak that it can only wail
The wreckage that strong hatred makes?
It shakes the earth,
And men's hearts fail
For fear of what it brings to birth,
The horror of great darkness — blood — and pain.
     Again — again

I see the proof that hate is strong
        And Love is weak;
The opposite of what I seek
Is round me everywhere,
To give the lie to all my dreams.
        If life be what it seems,
A slaughter-house and not a school,
An El Dorado where a fool
Is suffered to play havoc at his will,
        Can there be rest?
        Still—still
The endless, aimless struggle must go on,
And men, pale, haggard, wounded, wan,
Must stagger on to die,
And where they fall must lie
Unburied for the maggots and the flies,
Those hosts of flies;
        And the cries
Of men in agony
Must insult the summer skies,
And all the beauty of the world with doubt,
        Black doubt of God,
        Lest He who rules us with His rod
Be just a fiend of boundless cruelty,
        A demon in an angel's dress
        Who makes the world a wilderness
For His wild sport,
And laughs to see men caught
And torn to pieces in the meshes of His net:
        A God without regret,
Or bowels of compassion like a man.
        That doubt destroys all rest;
        It makes men weak,
        It bids them seek
        No longer—what is best,
But gather from the ruin what they can.

It starves the soul to selfishness
And bitter blank despair,
It taints the very air
            We breathe as do the dead,
            And all that we have read
            Of God in Christ seems lies,
            It makes us cynics,
And lays bare our souls for flies
            To fatten on—for lustings
            That wax gross and foul,
Like those great super-flies that buzz and prowl
About the long unburied carcass on the field.
            We are but weak, and yield
            Our best to their foul lips,
Our faith in Pity and our trust in Love.
            Doubt comes and grips
            Them by the throat and leaves them dead.
            The world seems red—blood red:
            How can we rest?
Come unto Me, He said.

            How can we come?   'Tis dark,
            So dark, the day has fled
And left a bloody trail back in the West.
            The way to Rest
            Is faint and hard to find,
            Like those dim tracks that wind
Across a dreary battlefield at night.
            Men travel round in circles and get lost,
            Come back to where two tracks had crossed
An hour ago,
            And so
In weary circles wend their way,
Still longing for the light,
Still calling in the night

To comrades wandering hopeless like themselves,
        Dim shapes that loom up sudden in the dark,
        And stand out black and stark
Against the sky.
They cry
        For guidance,
And perchance one thinks he knows
And goes,
Blind leader of the blind,
Down yet another track,
Which doubles and turns back
To where he started from,
And leaves the band of wanderers in the night.
        Such is our plight
        Who search for Thee
Across the bloody battlefields of Life.

Come unto Me:
It sounds like mockery,
A voice that calls a wounded man
        Across a weary space
He cannot travel o'er;
For we would come to Thee,
We long to see Thy face,
But we are wounded sore,
And evermore
Our weakness binds us,
Darkness blinds us,
We stretch our hands out vainly toward the shore,
Where Thou art waiting for Thine own.
We groan, and try, and fail again,
We cannot come—we are but men,
Come Thou to us, O Lord.
Come Thou and find us.
Shepherd of the sheep,
We cannot come to Thee.

It is so dark.
　　　But hark,
I hear a voice that sounds across the sea.
　　　"I come."

TWO WORLDS

In the valleys down below,
　　Where the fairest flowers blow,
And the brooks run babbling nonsense to the sea,
　　Underneath the shady trees,
　　We two sauntered at our ease,
Just a pleasant little world for you and me.

　　Then the summons of the Lord,
　　Like a sudden silver sword,
Came and cut our little pleasant world in two,
　　One fierce world of strife and hate,
　　One sad world where women wait,
And we wander far apart, dear, I and you.

　　And it may be, with this breath,
　　There will come the call of death,
And will put another world 'twixt you and me.
　　You will stand with God above,
　　I will stand 'twixt pride and Love,
Looking out through mists of sorrow o'er the sea.

　　Yet the world in God is one,
　　And when all our strife is done,
There will dawn the perfect world for you and me,
　　When we two together stand,
　　Looking upwards, hand in hand,
Where the fires of Love have burned up ev'ry sea.

WAIT

Silver clouds and a flying moon,
Wail, ye winds, to the reapers' tune
   For the dead white face upturned.
Two grey eyes, all dim with tears,
Bleak, how bleak are the barren years,
   When the fires of love are burned.
Two brave souls, and the great white King,
The end and the aim of everything
   Is the Peace of God well earned.

PARADISE

When machine-guns start to play
At the ending of the day,
And the sun's last burning ray
     Bleeds and dies.
When the sable warp of night
Is first cleft by silver light,
With its sudden curving flight
     Of surprise.
It is then that England calls
From its cottages and halls,
And we think of four dear walls
     And her eyes.
When the children's prayer is said,
And they lie tucked up in bed,
And the fire is burning red—
     Paradise.

ETERNAL HOPE

Can the Father in His Justice burn in everlasting flame
Souls that, sunk in foulest squalor, never knew the Father's
    Name?

Can the Love of man be greater than Eternal Love divine?
Can the heart of God be harder than this hardened heart of
    mine?

Can the pangs of Hell be endless, void of object, void of
    gain,
Save to pay for years of sorrow with Eternity of Pain?

Cursèd be the foul contortion, that hath turned His Love to
    Hate,
That hath cried at death's dim portal, "Enter here and 'tis
    too late."

Cruel pride and vain presumption claim to grasp where
    angels grope;
'Tis not God but mean man's blindness dims the deathless
    star of Hope.

DEAD AND BURIED

I have borne my cross through Flanders,
    Through the broken heart of France,
I have borne it through the deserts of the East;
    I have wandered, faint and longing,
    Through the human hosts that, thronging,
Swarmed to glut their grinning idols with a feast.

69

I was crucified in Cambrai,
And again outside Bapaume;
I was scourged for miles along the Albert Road,
I was driven, pierced and bleeding,
With a million maggots feeding
On the body that I carried as my load.

I have craved a cup of water,
Just a drop to quench my thirst,
As the routed armies ran to keep the pace;
But no soldier made reply
As the maddened hosts swept by,
And a sweating straggler kicked me in the face.

There's no ecstasy of torture
That the devils e'er devised,
That my soul has not endured unto the last;
As I bore my cross of sorrow,
For the glory of to-morrow,
Through the wilderness of battles that is past.

Yet my heart was still unbroken,
And my hope was still unquenched,
Till I bore my cross to Paris through the crowd.
Soldiers pierced me on the Aisne,
But 'twas by the river Seine
That the statesmen brake my legs and made my shroud.

There they wrapped my mangled body
In fine linen of fair words,
With the perfume of a sweetly scented lie,
And they laid it in the tomb
Of the golden-mirrored room,
'Mid the many-fountained Garden of Versailles.

With a thousand scraps of paper
They made fast the open door,
And the wise men of the Council saw it sealed.
With the seal of subtle lying
They made certain of my dying,
Lest the torment of the peoples should be healed.

Then they set a guard of soldiers
Night and day beside the Tomb,
Where the Body of the Prince of Peace is laid,
And the captains of the nations
Keep the sentries to their stations,
Lest the statesman's trust from Satan be betrayed.

For it isn't steel and iron
That men use to kill their God,
But the poison of a smooth and slimy tongue.
Steel and iron tear the body,
But it's oily sham and shoddy
That have trampled down God's *Spirit* in the dung.

DEMOBILISED

Out through its curtain of dark blue mist,
Glittering gold where the sun has kissed,
Out till it reaches the shining sea,
Stretches the land that is home to me;
Valley and hillock and wooded copse,
Promise of wealth in the fresh green crops.
Mother of Mothers that gave me birth,
Bone of my bone is thy rich red earth,
Flesh of my flesh is thy land to me,
The land that ends in the shining sea.

Mother, I come from a wounded land,
Where the earth is torn and the poor trees stand
Like naked masts, black—stiff—and stark,
Over the grave of some gallant bark;
Where peasant's cottage and nobles' halls
Are heaps of brick or the four bare walls,
With lonely graves in a maze of wire,
Where stood the church with its peaceful spire.
Out of the ruin I come to thee,
Hail, Mother mine, by the shining sea.

Dear to me ever thy country-side,
But dearer now for the men who died,
Robbed of the richest of youth's long years,
Steeling their hearts to a mother's tears,
Fighting their way through a thousand hells.
Bearing a cross like a cap and bells,
Jeering at death as a last good joke.
My thanks go up with the thin blue smoke.
Marking the cottage that's home to me,
In the dear safe land by the shining sea.

IF YE FORGET

Let me forget—Let me forget,
I am weary of remembrance,
And my brow is ever wet,
With tears of my remembrance,
With the tears and bloody sweat,—
    Let me forget.

If ye forget—If ye forget,
Then your children must remember,
And their brow be ever wet,

With the tears of their remembrance,
With the tears and bloody sweat, —
　　If ye forget.

AT A HARVEST FESTIVAL

Not here for high and holy things
　　We render thanks to Thee,
But for the common things of earth,
　　The purple pageantry
Of dawning and of dying days,
　　The splendour of the sea:

The royal robes of autumn moors,
　　The golden gates of spring,
The velvet of soft summer nights,
　　The silver glistering
Of all the million million stars,
　　The silent song they sing,

Of Faith and Hope and Love undimmed,
　　Undying still through death,
The Resurrection of the world,
　　What time there comes the breath
Of dawn that rustles through the trees,
　　And that clear voice that saith:

"Awake, awake to love and work,
　　The lark is in the sky,
The fields are wet with diamond dew,
　　The worlds awake to cry
Their blessings on the Lord of Life,
　　As He goes meekly by.

"Come, let thy voice be one with theirs,
   Shout with their shout of praise,
See how the giant sun soars up,
   Great Lord of years and days!
So let the Love of Jesus come,
   And set thy soul ablaze,

"To give and give, and give again,
   What God has given thee,
To spend thy self nor count the cost,
   To serve right gloriously
The God who gave all worlds that are,
   And all that are to be."

SO I DREAM

Nay, I know not what I dream of,
      Yet I dream.
Though my brow be ever wet
With the anguish and the sweat,
There is glory coming yet,
      Where the gleam
Leads me through the blinding mist,
By the way my Saviour wist,
To the shores that God has kissed, —
      So I dream.

There is more behind the sunshine
      Than the sun,
Fiercely flaming in the sky,
As the ages dawn and die,
Like a sneering sightless eye,
      Seeing none.
There's a voice my spirit knows,

In the sunset's gold and rose,
And the purple afterglows,
    When it's done.

There is speech behind the silence
    Of the night,
When the myriad array,
Sweeping down the Milky Way,
Marches on to dawning day
    Silver white;
When the velvet of the air,
Like some lovely woman's hair,
Drives the heavy eyes of care
    Out of sight.

There's a message in the music
    Of the deep,
When great Ocean's heaving swells,
Like God's big cathedral bells,
Boom their solemn-sounding knells,
    As they sweep,
In an ecstasy of pride,
At the flowing of the tide,
Over those who fought and died,
    Fast asleep.

There is love behind the splendour
    Of the spring,
When the weary winter dies
And the Lord with laughing eyes
Bids the trembling world arise,
    Whispering,
"Did ye think that God was dead?
Nay, my blood is warm and red,
And there is no death to dread—
    Come and sing."

Lord, I pray Thee give my spirit
    Eyes to see,
Through the things of time and space,
All the glories of Thy grace,
The commandment of Thy face,
    Bidding me
Follow on where Thou hast trod;
Though I share the grief of God,
Give me strength to sweat my blood,
    Lord, for Thee.

MY PEACE I LEAVE WITH YOU

Thy Peace!   Thou pale, despisèd Christ!
    What Peace is there in Thee,
Nailed to the Cross that crowns the world,
     In agony?

No Peace of home was Thine; no rest
    When Thy day's work was done.
When darkness called the world to sleep
    And veiled the sun,

No children gathered round Thy knee,
    No hand soothed care away:
Thou hadst not where to lay Thy head
    At close of day.

What Peace was Thine?   Misunderstood,
    Rejected by Thine own,
Pacing Thy grim Gethsemane,
    Outcast and lone.

What Peace hast Thou to give the world?
    There is enough of pain;
Always upon my window beats
        The sound of rain.

The source of sorrow is not dried,
    Nor stays the stream of tears,
But winds on weeping to the sea,
        All down the years.

For millions come to Golgotha
    To suffer and to die,
Forsaken in their hour of need,
        And asking, Why?

Man's Via Crucis never ends,
    Earth's Calvaries increase,
The world is full of spears and nails,
        But where is Peace?

"Take up Thy Cross and follow Me,
    I am the Way, my son,
Via Crucis, Via Pacis,
        Meet and are one."

APRIL

Breath of Spring,
Not come, but coming,
In the air.
Life of earth, not lived
But living,
Everywhere.
Promises, not made,
Nor broken,

But the token
Of promises that will be made.
Sunshine seeking shade,
Red earth, that smiles,
And asks for seed,
And mossy woodland paths, that lead
To where the yellow primrose grows.
And so for many coloured miles
Of open smiling France,
While noisy little streamlets dance,
In diamond mirrored suns,
To meet the stately Mother stream that flows,
With shining dignity,
To greet her Lord the sea,
And far away, beyond the hills, one hears,
—Poor village Mother, hence thy tears!—
The muffled thunder of the guns.

"THE ENDING OF THE DAY"

Toil is over,
Scent of clover
Wafts along the western way.
Farewell sorrow,
Till to-morrow,
'Tis the ending of the day.

Shyly, sweetly,
So discreetly,
Smiles my Love nor says me nay.
Darling, this is
Time for kisses,
'Tis the ending of the day.

Silvery moonshine,
All the world mine,
Drink we Love's wine while we may,
Time is flying,
Leaves are dying,
'Tis the ending of the day.

Love is sweetest,
Frailest, fleetest,
Of the joys that will not stay;
Kisses deeper
Cannot keep her,
'Tis the ending of the day.

Life is over,
Dead the clover,
All the world is growing grey;
Barren blisses,
Colder kisses,
'Tis the ending of the day.

A SCRAP OF PAPER

Just a little scrap of paper
In a yellow envelope,
And the whole world is a ruin,
Even Hope.

MISSING—BELIEVED KILLED

On reading a Mother's Letter

'Twere heaven enough to fill my heart
  If only one would stay,
Just one of all the million joys
  God gives to take away.

If I could keep one golden dawn,
  The splendour of one star,
One silver glint of yon bird's wing
  That flashes from afar;

If I could keep the least of things
  That make me catch my breath
To gasp with wonder at God's world.
  And hold it back from death,

It were enough; but death forbids.
  The sunset flames to fade,
The velvet petals of this rose
  Fall withered—brown—decayed.

She only asked to keep one thing,
  The joy-light in his eyes:
God has not even let her know
  Where his dead body lies.

O Grave, where is thy victory?
  O Death, where is thy sting?
Thy victory is ev'rywhere,
  Thy sting's in ev'rything.

CHEER-I-O!

Here's to you and here's to me,
Here's to pals on land and sea,
Here's to Peace that is to be,
    Cheer-i-o!

Here's to those who live and fight,
Here's to those gone out of sight,
Who have fought and died for Right,
    Cheer-i-o!
    Cheer-i-o! Cheer-i-o!

On we'll go through weal or woe,
On through any blinkin' show,
    Cheer-i-o!

It's the battle-cry of God,
As He works in star and sod,
Beating Satan with His rod,
    Cheer-i-o!

It's the cry that made the earth,
Gave the rolling spheres their birth,
Wrought a world of wondrous worth,
    Cheer-i-o!

If it comes my turn to die,
To be outed and put by,
May I peg out with this cry,
    Cheer-i-o!

TO PATRICK

I gave thee life, my little son,
  And thou art part of me;
Which part? Would God I knew the Truth,
  Then were my soul set free
From fretting fears all down the years,
  From dull anxiety;

Lest I have given thee that part,
  Which makes my angel weep,
That underworld whence lusts and lies,
  Like vermin, crawl and creep
Across my visions and my prayers;
  Whence selfish passions leap

To slay the very thing I love,
  To crucify my Lord,
To strangle Jesus in my soul,
  With coils of evil cord,
And force me spit my sins upon
  The face my soul adored.

Fain would I give thee those bright wings
  On which my spirit flies,
To talk with angels on the heights,
  In solemn sweet surprise,
And win from Him, who is the Light,
  The poet's open eyes.

IT IS FINISHED

It is finished! It is finished! as the sun sinks down to
rest,
And the sky burns blood and amber in the wonder-weaving
West,
Where the clouds make golden islands like the Islands of
the Blest,
       For the day is nearly done.

But another day is dawning as the wingèd darkness
flies,
And the silver stars keep sentry till another sun shall
rise,
For the daylight is eternal, and the sunshine never dies,
       It is always marching on.

It is finished! It is finished! for the Saviour crucified,
See the soldiers stand in silence where the cruel crowds
have cried,
E'en the broken-hearted mother has departed from His
side,
       For His day is nearly done.

But an empty tomb is waiting, and the East is silver grey,
As the angels of the morning trumpet in another day,
See the wounded God go walking down the world's eternal
way,
       For His task is never done.

There's an army thronging round Him as He takes the road
to-night,
Can't you see your sons and brothers lined before Him left
and right?

Can't you hear their voices calling you to join the host and
        fight
                For the God who marches on?

                        TRUTH

                Sunshine and shadow,
                And their strife,
                Is that indeed the lot in life
                That God has meted to the sons of men?
                Through yon gold mist,
                That God has kissed,
                And waked to greater glory than the day,
                Is that the way
                By which we climb up to the final place,
                And see God's face
                Burn through the shadows at the last?
                It has been so,
                That much we know,
                That is the very message of man's past;
                We know in part,
                But still the heart
                Of very Truth seems far away.
                Time turns our Truth to falsehood,
                And a brighter day
                Makes evening of our morning;
                And round us once again the shadows lie,
                And hide the sun.
                Our search is never done.
                We stumble onward toward that light,
                Too bright
                For us to see unshadowed, lest we die.
                O God, if that be life,
                To take this strife,

                        84

And keep it up unbeaten to the end,
Then, God of mercy, send
One ray
Of Thine own glory-light
To touch our world to-day
The shadows have departed,
And black night
Lies brooding over all the earth,
And hideous things find birth.
The world brings forth abortions,
And then weeps bloody tears,
Because her womb is shamed,
Her children maimed,
And all her home become a wilderness of sin.
The sun is darkened,
And the moon turned into blood,
And down upon us sweeps a flood
Of Lust and Cruelty.
 God sleeps;
Or is He dead,
And all that we have read
Of His great Love a lie,
That must be buried with the others in the past,
The last—the very last
Sweet lie that we shall ever have,
To keep us from despair, which is the Truth,
The cruel Truth?
More Light—more Light!
O God of Life, one Breath
 Of air,
Or else we die!
The shadows conquer,
And we lie in darkness,
Darkness of despair,
 Which is the second death.

. . . .

But look, the shadows weaken,
And the sun beats through;
'Tis true—God lives—I knew.
I think I always knew!

IT IS NOT FINISHED

It is not finished, Lord.
There is not one thing done,
There is no battle of my life,
That I have really won.
And now I come to tell Thee
How I fought to fail,
My human, all too human, tale
Of weakness and futility.
And yet there is a faith in me,
That Thou wilt find in it
One word that Thou canst take
And make
The centre of a sentence
In Thy book of poetry.
I cannot read this writing of the years,
My eyes are full of tears,
It gets all blurred, and won't make sense
It's full of contradictions
Like the scribblings of a child,
Such wild, wild
Hopes, and longing as intense
As pain, which trivial deeds
Make folly of—or worse:
I can but hand it in, and hope
That Thy great mind, which reads
The writings of so many lives,
Will understand this scrawl

And what it strives
To say—but leaves unsaid.
I cannot write it over,
The stars are coming out,
My body needs its bed.
I have no strength for more,
So it must stand or fall—Dear Lord—
  That's all.

GOOD FRIDAY FALLS ON
LADY DAY

And has our Lady lost Her place?
 Does Her white Star burn dim?
Nay, She has lowly veiled Her face
 Because of Him.

Men give to Her the jewelled crown,
 And robe with broidered rim,
But fain is She to cast them down
 Because of Him.

She claims no crown from Christ apart,
 Who gave God life and limb,
She only claims a broken heart
 Because of Him.

THEN WILL HE COME

When through the whirl of wheels and engines humming,
 Patient in power for the sons of men,

Peals like a trumpet promise of His coming,
    Who in the clouds is pledged to come again.

When through the night the furnace fires flaring,
    Loud with their tongues of flame like spurting blood,
Speak to the heart of love alive and daring,
    Sing of the boundless energy of God.

When in the depths the patient miner striving,
    Feels in his arms the vigour of the Lord,
Strikes for a kingdom and his kings arriving,
    Holding his pick more splendid than the sword.

When on the sweat of labour and its sorrow,
    Toiling in twilight, flickering and dim,
Flames out the sunshine of the great to-morrow,
    When all the world looks up—because of Him.

Then will He come—with meekness for His glory,
    God in a workman's jacket as before,
Living again the Eternal Gospel Story,
    Sweeping the shavings from His workshop floor.

THE UNUTTERABLE BEAUTY

    God, give me speech, in mercy touch my lips,
    I cannot bear Thy Beauty and be still,
    Watching the red-gold majesty that tips
        The crest of yonder hill,
    And out to sea smites on the sails of ships,

    That flame like drifting stars across the deep,
    Calling their silver comrades from the sky,
    As long and ever longer shadows creep,

To sing their lullaby,
And hush the tired eyes of earth to sleep.

Thy radiancy of glory strikes me dumb,
Yet cries within my soul for power to raise
Such miracles of music as would sum
Thy splendour in a phrase,
Storing it safe for all the years to come.

O God, Who givest songs too sweet to sing,
Have mercy on Thy servant's feeble tongue,
In sacrificial silence sorrowing,
And grant that songs unsung,
Accepted at Thy mercy-seat, may bring

New light into the darkness of sad eyes,
New tenderness to stay the stream of tears,
New rainbows from the sunshine of surprise,
To guide men down the years,
Until they cross the last long bridge of sighs.

THE SOUL OF DOUBT

That's it.   Doubt's very soul of doubt
Lies here.   Is God just faith in God,
Or can God work His will without
Our human faith?   Is flesh and blood
Made by, or maker of, the mind
That works upon the mass of things
Inanimate?   Has this wild wind
A master, riding on its wings
His chosen way, or is it free
Of any but its own mad will
To sweep in wanton liberty

Over the patient earth, and spill
Destruction, breaking hearts and homes,
A drunken thing without a plan
Or purpose anywhere?   It comes
To that at last.   Is mortal man
Fated to fight a senseless world
Of blind material force alone,
By its haphazard powers hurled
This way and that, until his own
Small wit in desperation finds
A way to short uncertain Peace?
Around this core of doubt thought winds
Its endless coil, seeking release,
And, finding none, for ever binds
Its meshes tighter round the soul.

.   .   .   .   .

The preachers blame our lack of faith
For all our human ills, but why?
Does God depend on man?   "Thus saith
The Lord omnipotent," they cry.
Aye, God for ever says, but we
Must do, and how?   We lack the power,
And from the task's immensity
Reel back in fear, as hour by hour
It grows, and frowning peak on peak
The evil mountains rise ahead.
We stumble on bewildered, weak,
Half blind, trusting what we have read
Of God, that legendary Love
Urgent to help us, and redeem
Our souls, a Love we cannot prove,
But shut out aching eyes and dream
It true.   Could any God endure
The sight unmoved and silent still?
Would not a real God assure

Our doubts, and work His mighty Will
Without our faith? So many wrecks;
Wrecked faith, wrecked hope, wrecked love,
    wrecked dreams;
And still we bow our helpless necks
To meet the storm. God's silence seems
Decisive. God is only faith
In God, and when Faith dies, God dies,
And Hope, a homeless weeping wraith,
Beats on her shrivelled breasts, and cries,
Refusing to be comforted,
Because her little ones are dead,
All dead.
And yet—and yet—doubt may deceive,
Joy may give truer thought than grief.
It may be so, Lord, I believe,
In mercy help mine unbelief.

REALISM

This poet parasite of grief
Lives on the falling, leaf by leaf,
Of Life's illusion, glad to see
The nakedness of misery.
He probes his pen deep down within,
To make a sonnet of a sin,
A realist revealing less
Of beauty than of bitterness.
Yet purer eyes than his have seen
Truth in these fields of living green,
And truer hearts than his have trod
White ways of wonder up to God.
Lord, touch my lips that I may sing

91

The music of man's hallowing;
Touch Thou my soul that I may know
Life's worth more real than its woe.

EASTER HYMN

Lord, our land is stricken sore,
Raging torrents are its rills,
There is snow upon the moor,
Snow upon the lonely hills;
Bitter wails the northern blast,
Blinding sleet is in our eyes,
Clutched by icy fingers fast,
Pity our captivities.

Come, Thou Conqu'ring Saviour, come,
Sound Thy silver clarion loud,
Rise, and lead Thy children home,
Rend the warp of winter's shroud.
Speak, and by Thy living breath,
Stay the land's long harrowing,
Smite the scornful hosts of death
With the sudden sword of spring.

Let Thy streams of mercy blend,
Bringing Peace without, within,
Let the night of nature end
With the longer night of sin.
Let two worlds awake and cry,
Spring has come and winter fled,
Dark is over, dawn is nigh,
Christ is Risen from the dead.

TO CHRISTOPHER

Bear Thou the Christ,
My little son.
He will not burden Thee.
That Holy One.
For, by a mystery,
Who bearest Him He bears
Eternally,
Up to the radiant heights
Where Angels be,
And heaven's crimson crown of lights
Flames round the crystal sea.

TRUTH'S BETRAYAL

Oft have I sat with kindred spirits, weaving
Webs of fine reason proving Him divine
Far thro' the night, and waked to my deceiving,
Fooled by a pride intoxicant as wine.

Pride in the power to follow thro' the mazes,
Winding the threads of logic in and out,
Pride in the shallow paradox of phrases
Coined in a flash to put a truth to rout.

Swiftly they come full-armed for His betraying,
Traitorous kisses on the lips of thought,
Shaming the Christ by subtlety of saying,
Careless to sell sincerity for nought.

Not to the wise, O Lord, nor to the prudent,
  Dost Thou reveal Thyself, nor to the art
Of the logician keen, and coldly student,
  But to the patience of the pure in heart.

Low is the lintel of Thy Truth, and lowly
  Mortals must bend who fain would see Thy face.
Slow from the darkness dawns the day, and slowly
  Sinners ascend into Thy dwelling-place.

THE SONG OF SILENCE

If I with tongue from trembling free,
My soul pure white as under-snows,
Could sweep God's heart-strings, and compose
    The melody

That silence sings to this soft night,
Brooding upon the purple hills,
And whispers to the daffodils
    So tall and white

Beneath the moon, their colour fled,
Like vestal virgins in a trance,
Pure heroines of God's romance
    All hallowèd;

If I could make that music mine,
'Twould swell into a perfect song,
Drowning the world's discordant wrong
    In strains divine.

Strong saints would sell their souls to hear,
And lovers pay a broken kiss
To taste a sweetness such as this.
        Without a tear,

Mothers would leave the worshipping
Of baby lips and baby eyes,
And smile in exquisite surprise
        To hear me sing.

All flesh would follow where I trod,
And, with one single starlit mind,
Would hie them forth to seek, and find
        The Voice of God.

TRAGEDY

I know.   It is not easy to explain
Why should there be such agony to bear?
Why should the whole wide world be full of pain?
But then, why should her hair
Be like the sudden sunshine after rain?

Turn cynic if you will.   Curse God and die.
You've ample reason for it.   There's enough
Of bitterness, God knows, to answer why.
The road of life is rough,
But then there is the glory of the sky.

I find it ever thus.   I scorn the sun.
I con the book of years in bitter rage.
I swear that faith in God is dead and done,
But then I turn a page,
And shake my sides with laughter at His fun.

If life were only tragedy all through,
And I could play some high heroic part,
With fate and evil furies to pursue,
I would with steadfast heart,
But my fine tragic parts are never true.

God always laughs and spoils them, and for me
He sets the stage to suit a human fool,
Who blunders in where angels fear to be,
So if life is His School,
I trow He means to teach Humility.

I AND MY ROSE

There is a world of wonder in this rose;
God made it, and His whole creation grows
To a point of perfect beauty
In this garden plot.   He knows
The poet's thrill
On this June morning, as He sees
His Will
To beauty taking form, His word
Made flesh, and dwelling among men.
All mysteries
In this one flower meet
And intertwine,
The universal is concrete
The human and divine,
In one unique and perfect thing, are fused
Into a unity of Love,
This rose as I behold it;
For all things gave it me,
The stars have helped to mould it,
The air, soft moonshine, and the rain,

The meekness of old mother earth,
The many-billowed sea.
The evolution of ten million years,
And all the pain
Of ages, brought it to its birth
And gave it me.
The tears
Of Christ are in it,
And His Blood
Has dyed it red,
I could not see it but for Him
Because He led
Me to the Love of God,
From which all Beauty springs.
I and my rose
Are one.

I LOST MY LORD

I lost my Lord and sought Him long,
    I journeyed far, and cried
His name to every wand'ring wind,
    But still my Lord did hide.

I sought Him in the stately shrines,
    Where priest and people pray,
But empty went my spirit in
    And empty turned away.

I sought Him where the Doctors meet
    To turn deep questions o'er,
But every answer tempted me
    To ask one question more.

I sought Him where the hermit kneels
　　And tells his beads of pain.
I found Him with some children here
　　In this green Devon lane.

I WILL LIFT UP MY EYES . . .

Up to these purple hills, O God,
　　I lift my longing eyes,
Thy gaunt and silent sentinels
　　Against the sunset skies;

Their great heads bowed upon their breasts,
　　Their helmets tipped with flame,
They stand to guard the mystery
　　Of Thy most Holy Name.

All gnarled but empty are their hands,
　　They wield nor sword nor spear,
And yet in trembling reverence
　　My stubborn soul draws near.

Their awful silence breaks my heart,
　　This patience of the years,
The challenge of eternity
　　To tide of time and tears.

The paltry prizes of my sin
　　Show shameful, poor, and mean,
O mercifully merciless,
　　Unclean! I am unclean!

O God, whose dread is on the hills!
　　I dare not come to Thee,
I can but beat upon my breast
　　And clutch at Calvary.

WORK

Close by the careless worker's side,
    Still patient stands
The Carpenter of Nazareth,
    With piercèd hands
Outstretched to plead unceasingly,
    His Love's demands.

Longing to pick the hammer up
    And strike a blow,
Longing to feel His plane swing out,
    Steady and slow,
The fragrant shavings falling down,
    Silent as snow.

Because this is my Work, O Lord,
    It must be Thine,
Because it is a human task
    It is divine.
Take me, and brand me with Thy Cross,
    Thy slave's proud sign.

THE COLLIERS' HYMN

Now praisèd be the Lord our God
    Whose Love is living flame,
Who rules the ages with His rod,
    For wondrous is His Name.

Who, ere His children came to birth
    Prepared this vasty deep,

And stored within the womb of earth
   Ten million suns to sleep.

Fierce noontides of forgotten years
   Around us glint and gleam,
The glory of the Lord appears
   Black seam upon black seam.

O God of all the depths and heights,
   Thou Father of man's soul,
Clear is Thy Love on starry nights,
   Clear in the shining coal.

By all the colliers' blood and sweat,
   By collier woman's tears,
By all the sin that men forget,
   Of those accursèd years.

When martyred children crawled and cried,
   Black slaves to buy and sell,
By cruel men despised, denied,
   Naked and lost in hell.

Have mercy on Thy people, Lord,
   Bid deeds of darkness cease,
Unsheathe Love's sunshine as a sword
   And in the pit give Peace.

LIGHTEN OUR DARKNESS

Lighten our darkness, Lord, in bygone years,
Oft have I prayed and thought on childish fears,
Glad in my heart that, when the day was dead,
God's four white angels watched about my bed.

Lighten our darkness! Kneeling in the mud,
My hands still wet and warm with human blood,
Oft have I prayed it! Perils of this night!
Sorrow of soldiers! Mercy, give us light.

Lighten our darkness! Black upon the mind
Questions and doubts, so many paths that wind,
Worlds of blind sorrow crying out for sight.
Peace, where is Peace? Lord Jesus, give us light.

Lighten our darkness! Stumbling to the end,
Millions of mortals feeling for a friend,
Shall not the Judge of all the earth do right?
Flame through the darkness, Lord, and give us Light.

IF I HAD A MILLION POUNDS

I would buy me a perfect island home,
   Sweet set in a southern sea,
And there would I build me a paradise
   For the heart o' my Love and me.

I would plant me a perfect garden there,
   The one that my dream soul knows,
And the years would flow as the petals grow,
   That flame to a perfect rose.

I would build me a perfect temple there,
   A shrine where my Christ might dwell,
And then would I wake to behold my soul
   Damned deep in a perfect Hell.

THE COWARD PILGRIM

It is too far away;
It were presumption to suppose the span
Of our poor human life were long enough
To travel there.   Let us then wait God's time,
And when our little evening fades away
To darken into night of death, we shall
Awake to find ourselves within its gates.
So many have set out and fallen faint
And weary by the way; so many saints
Have left their bones to witness how they failed;
Shall we poor sinners then succeed?   Vain hope!
It is not for this world, nor of this world,
That Kingdom of the Christ.   It lies beyond
The mountains, where the sun of this life sets.

So coward pilgrims talk
To comfort their faint hearts, and soothe to peace
Uneasy consciences that call within
And bid them rise, awake, and walk the way,
The steep white way of wonder, up to God.
It is not far—'tis but a little way,
But steep, over the hill of Calvary
And through the Garden, where the tomb, rock-hewn,
Stands empty, with a great stone rolled aside.
There lies the pilgrim path by which He went,
That first great Pilgrim, blazing out the trail
By Blood of Sacrifice.   There still He stands,
And calls: I am the Way—the Truth—the Life;
O ye of little faith!   Arise and walk!
Am I not with you always as ye climb?

THE CHALLENGE

Can'st Thou drink the cup I drank of?
Can'st thou bear to be baptized
With the baptism of bitterness and Truth?
Can'st thou see thy dreams all dying,
And thy hopes around thee lying
In a ruin, and retain the eyes of youth?

Can'st thou hear the Siren's calling
And stand firm, with strong men falling?
Can'st defy the sons of Belial running wild?
Can'st thou see Love's honour slighted,
And its fairest blossom blighted,
And live on, still looking forward like a child?

Then arise, my knight defender,
Be thou terrible and tender,
In the strength that down the ages has sufficed,
And, in scorn of all their scorning,
Seek the splendour of the morning,
When the darkness shall be shattered by the Christ

IT'S HARD TO BE A
CARPENTER

I wonder what He charged for chairs
At Nazareth.
And did men try to beat Him down,
And boast about it in the town,
"I bought it cheap for half a crown
From that mad carpenter"?

And did they promise and not pay,
Put it off to another day,
O did they break His heart that way,
My Lord the Carpenter?
I wonder did He have bad debts,
And did He know my fears and frets?
The Gospel writer here forgets
To tell about the Carpenter.
But that's just what I want to know.
Ah! Christ in glory, here below
Men cheat and lie to one another so
It's hard to be a carpenter.

HE WAS A GAMBLER TOO . . .

And, sitting down, they watched Him there,
The soldiers did;
There, while they played with dice,
He made His Sacrifice,
And died upon the Cross to rid
God's world of sin.
He was a gambler too, my Christ,
He took His life and threw
It for a world redeemed.
And ere His agony was done,
Before the westering sun went down,
Crowning that day with its crimson crown,
He knew that He had won.

BECAUSE I LOVE HIM SO . . .

She could not follow where He went,
   She could but watch Him go,
And bless Him, though her heart was rent
   Because she loved Him so.

She stood once at a cottage door,
   To watch His figure grow
Distant and dim, heart-sore, heart-sore,
   Because she loved Him so.

She had to turn from Calvary,
   Turn when He bade her go,
Leaving her heart nailed to the Tree,
   Because she loved Him so.

Mother of Jesus, Holy One,
   My sorrows thou dost know;
Bless Thou my son, my little son,
   Because I love him so.

THE EAST WINDOW

There is a little church here old and grey,
By red-green cliffs that smiling kiss the sea,
And, through its eastern window, each new day
Reveals a mystery,
The Truth of Beauty — the eternal way

Of Love.   A butterfly with wings outspread
As though for flight, but at its heart a cross,

Whereon the perfect Lover bows His head,
While Mary mourns the loss
Of her dear Beauty bleeding, bruised, and dead.

Yet Beauty lives, as dawn on dawn burns through,
Making a royal splendour of His pain.
The butterfly revives, gold, crimson, blue,
He moves his wings again,
All wonderful and wet with morning dew,

And takes his flight.   The Beauty that man slays,
By grasping at it ruthless in his greed,
Is dead, until the Lover comes and pays
The price with hands that bleed,
And makes of it a soaring song of praise.

CHRISTMAS CAROL

Come worship the King,
That little white thing,
Asleep on His Mother's soft breast.
Ye bright stars, bow down,
Weave for Him a crown,
Christ Jesus by angels confessed.

Come, children, and peep,
But hush ye, and creep
On tiptoe to where the Babe lies;
Then whisper His Name
And lo! like a flame
The Glory light shines in His eyes.

Come, strong men, and see
This high mystery,
Tread firm where the shepherds have trod,

And watch, 'mid the hair
Of the Maiden so fair,
The five little fingers of God.

Come, old men and grey,
The star leads the way,
It halts, and your wanderings cease;
Look down on His Face,
Then, filled with His Grace,
Depart ye, God's servants, in Peace.

THE PSYCHOLOGIST

He takes the saints to pieces,
And labels all the parts,
He tabulates the secrets
Of loyal loving hearts.
He probes their selfless passion,
And shows exactly why
The martyr goes out singing,
To suffer and to die.
The beatific vision
That brings them to their knees
He smilingly reduces
To infant phantasies.
The Freudian unconscious
Quite easily explains
The splendour of their sorrows,
The pageant of their pains.
The manifold temptations,
Wherewith the flesh can vex
The saintly soul, are samples
Of Œdipus complex.

The subtle sex perversion,
    His eagle glance can tell,
That makes their joyous heaven
    The horror of their hell.
His reasoning is perfect,
    His proofs as plain as paint,
He has but one small weakness,
    He cannot make a saint.

BROWN EYES

Her eyes are brown,
Soft brown, like autumn leaves
Cast down,
Wherewith the wise Pan weaves

His carpeting
For winter woods.   They keep
Sweet spring,
Rapt in her beauty sleep,

Until she smiles,
Then sudden swift surprise
Beguiles
My soul to Paradise,

And passion wakes
To grasp, but waits to pray,
Forsakes
Itself, and finds Love's way.

SURSUM CORDA

There are cowslips in the clearing,
   With God's green and gold ablaze,
And the distant hills are nearing,
   Through a sun-kissed sea of haze.

There's a lilt of silver laughter
   In the brook upon its way,
With the sunbeams stumbling after
   Like the children at their play.

There's a distant cuckoo calling
   To the lark up in the sky
As his song comes falling, falling
   To his nest—a happy sigh.

Sursum Corda! How the song swells
   From the woods that smile and nod.
Sursum Corda! Ring the bluebells,
   Lift ye up your hearts to God.

LOVE'S DAWN

I never loved thee, mine, until these tears
Of common sorrow bound us into one.
Then when we danced together down the years,
And shouted in the sun,
Greeting the dawn of each new day with cheers,

We were not one.   Our souls were still asleep,
We were companions in a childish game,
Until the great God called and bade us weep,
Until the darkness came,
And we went hand in hand down to the deep.

Then were we naked both and unashamed,
Soul clave to soul stripped of the clinging flesh,
Till out of sorrow's heart pure passion flamed
To incarnate afresh
Two spirits in the body Love reclaimed.

There 'neath the starless skies our souls embraced,
And of their true compassion joy was born,
Then, on the awful verge of that grey waste,
The fingers of the morn
In blood-red letters their new message traced.

THERE SHALL BE LIGHT

Red royal of the Devon cliffs
    Slashed with their glowing green,
Fast-fading purple in the West,
    The silver moon serene,
And climbing up to call the stars,
    O Love that might have been.

This lonely beauty is such pain,
    It hurts and cannot heal,
It can but set upon the soul
    The crowning sorrow's seal,
And leave it crying out for death,
    For Peace that cannot feel.

Yet would I live and keep my pain,
    Nor barter it for bliss.
The sunset is not all farewell,
    There's promise in its kiss,
Of deathless dawn that is to break
    On Beauty such as this.

TAKE HEED HOW YE DESPISE

Thou who art Lord of all the tender pities,
    Mercy Incarnate, human and divine,
How can we write Thy name upon these cities
    Wherein Thy children live like herded swine?

Would not those eyes, that saw their angels gazing
    Into the brightness of the Father's face,
Turn on this slum with Love and fury blazing,
    Shriv'ling our souls with shame of such a place?

"Where are My children, those the Father gave you?
    What have you done with babes that bore My name?
Was it for this I suffered so to save you?
    Must I for ever burn for you in shame?"

BUILDERS

We shall build on!
We shall build on!
On through the cynic's scorning,

111

On through the coward's warning,
On through the cheat's suborning,
        We shall build on!
Firm on the Rock of Ages,
City of saints and sages,
Laugh while the tempest rages,
        We shall build on!
Christ, though my hands be bleeding,
Fierce though my flesh be pleading,
Still let me see Thee leading,
        Let me build on!
Till through death's cruel dealing,
Brain wrecked and reason reeling,
I hear Love's trumpets pealing,
        And I pass on.

THE JUDGE

Methought it was the end of time,
    The dawn of judgment day,
The world stood waiting for the judge,
    Dim faces drawn and grey.

The sword of dawn slashed thro' the East,
    I did not dare to see,
But threw my arm across my face
    From that dread mystery.

Then trembling raised reluctant eyes,
    To look upon the throne,
But all the earth was emptiness,
    And I stood all alone.

Till I looked down, and at my feet,
    With shining eyes and mild,
And two small wounded hands held out,
    There stood my Judge — a Child.

MARCHING SONG

I can hear the steady tramping of a thousand thousand
    feet,
Making music in the city and the crowded village street,
I can see a million mothers with their hands outstretched to
    greet,
        For the army's marching home.

I can see a million visions that are dancing overhead
Of the glory that is dawning where the sky is burning red,
Of the Britain to be builded for the honour of the dead,
        For the army's marching home.

I can see the broken women choking back their scalding
    tears,
Oh! the barren, empty greyness of their lonely, loveless
    years!
But their duty's to the living and they'll only give them
    cheers,
        As the army marches home.

I can see a crowd of children on the crest of yonder hill,
I can hear their little voices cheering, cheering loud and
    shrill,
'Tis that they may grow to beauty that our flag is floating
    still,
        As the army marches home.

There's a crowd of wooden crosses in the wounded heart
of France,
Where the cornfields used to glisten and the blood-red
poppies dance,
Can't you hear the crosses calling us to give the Christ a
chance,
      Now the army's marching home?

O! we'll build a mighty temple for the lowly Prince of
Peace,
And the splendour of its beauty shall compel all wars to
cease.
There the weak shall find a comrade and the captive find
release,
      When the army marches home.

Of men's hearts it shall be builded, and of spirits tried and
true,
And its courts shall know no bound'ries save the bound'ries
of the blue,
And it's there we shall remember those who died for me
and you,
      When the army has marched home.

DIALECT POEMS

THE SORROW OF GOD

A Sermon in a Billet

Yes, I used to believe i' Jesus Christ,
    And I used to go to Church,
But sin' I left 'ome and came to France,
    I've been clean knocked off my perch.
For it seemed orlright at 'ome, it did,
    To believe in a God above
And in Jesus Christ 'Is only Son,
    What died on the Cross through Love.
When I went for a walk o' a Sunday morn
    On a nice fine day in the spring,
I could see the proof o' the living God
    In every living thing.
For 'ow could the grass and the trees grow up
    All along o' their bloomin' selves?
Ye might as well believe i' the fairy tales,
    And think they was made by elves.
So I thought as that long-'aired atheist
    Were nubbat a silly sod,
For 'ow did 'e 'count for my Brussels sprouts
    If 'e didn't believe i' God?
But it ain't the same out 'ere, ye know.
    It's as different as chalk fro' cheese,
For 'arf on it's blood and t'other 'arf's mud,
    And I'm damned if I really sees
'Ow the God, who 'as made such a cruel world,
    Can 'ave Love in 'Is 'eart for men,

And be deaf to the cries of the men as dies
    And never comes 'ome again.
Just look at that little boy corporal there,
    Such a fine upstanding lad,
Wi' a will uv 'is own, and a way uv 'is own,
    And a smile uv 'is own, 'e 'ad.
An hour ago 'e were bustin' wi' life,
    Wi' 'is actin' and foolin' and fun;
'E were simply the life on us all, 'e were,
    Now look what the blighters 'a done.
Look at 'im lyin' there all uv a 'eap,
    Wi' the blood soaken over 'is 'ead,
Like a beautiful picture spoiled by a fool,
    A bundle o' nothin'—dead.
And it ain't only 'im—there's a mother at 'ome,
    And 'e were the pride of 'er life.
For it's women as pays in a thousand ways
    For the madness o' this 'ere strife.
And the lovin' God 'E looks down on it all,
    On the blood and the mud and the smell.
O God, if it's true, 'ow I pities you,
    For ye must be livin' i' 'ell.
You must be livin' i' 'ell all day,
    And livin' i' 'ell all night.
I'd rather be dead, wiv a 'ole through my 'ead,
    I would, by a damn long sight,
Than be livin' wi' you on your 'eavenly throne,
    Lookin' down on yon bloody 'eap
That were once a boy full o' life and joy,
    And 'earin' 'is mother weep.
The sorrows o' God must be 'ard to bear
    If 'E really 'as Love in 'Is 'eart,
And the 'ardest part i' the world to play
    Must surely be God's part.
And I wonder if that's what it really means,
    That Figure what 'angs on the Cross.

116

I remember I seed one t'other day
    As I stood wi' the captain's 'oss.
I remember, I thinks, thinks I to mysel',
    It's a long time since 'E died,
Yet the world don't seem much better to-day
    Then when 'E were crucified.
It's allus the same, as it seems to me,
    The weakest must go to the wall,
And whether 'e's right, or whether 'e's wrong,
    It don't seem to matter at all.
The better ye are and the 'arder it is,
    The 'arder ye 'ave to fight,
It's a cruel 'ard world for any bloke
    What does the thing as is right.
And that's 'ow 'E came to be crucified,
    For that's what 'E tried to do.
'E were allus a-tryin' to do 'Is best
    For the likes o' me and you.
Well, what if 'E came to the earth to-day,
    Came walkin' about this trench,
'Ow 'Is 'eart would bleed for the sights 'E seed,
    I' the mud and the blood and the stench.
And I guess it would finish 'Im up for good
    When 'E came to this old sap end,
And 'E seed that bundle o' nothin' there,
    For 'E wept at the grave uv 'Is friend.
And they say 'E were just the image o' God.
    I wonder if God sheds tears,
I wonder if God can be sorrowin' still,
    And 'as been all these years.
I wonder if that's what it really means,
    Not only that 'E once died,
Not only that 'E came once to the earth
    And wept and were crucified?
Not just that 'E suffered once for all
    To save us from our sins,

And then went up to 'Is throne on 'igh
　　To wait till 'Is 'eaven begins.
But what if 'E came to the earth to show,
　　By the paths o' pain that 'E trod,
The blistering flame of eternal shame
　　That burns in the heart o' God?
O God, if that's 'ow it really is,
　　Why, bless ye, I understands,
And I feels for you wi' your thorn-crowned 'ead
　　And your ever piercèd 'ands.
But why don't ye bust the show to bits,
　　And force us to do your will?
Why ever should God be suffering so
　　And man be sinning still?
Why don't ye make your voice ring out,
　　And drown these cursèd guns?
Why don't ye stand with an outstretched 'and,
　　Out there 'twixt us and the 'Uns?
Why don't ye force us to end the war
　　And fix up a lasting peace?
Why don't ye will that the world be still
　　And wars for ever cease?
That's what I'd do, if I was you,
　　And I had a lot o' sons
What squabbled and fought and spoilt their 'ome,
　　Same as us boys and the 'Uns.
And yet, I remember, a lad o' mine,
　　'E's fightin' now on the sea,
And 'e were a thorn in 'is mother's side,
　　And the plague o' my life to me.
Lord, 'ow I used to swish that lad
　　Till 'e fairly yelped wi' pain,
But fast as I thrashed one devil out
　　Another popped in again.
And at last, when 'e grew up a strappin' lad,
　　'E ups and 'e says to me,

"My will's my own and my life's my own,
  And I'm goin', Dad, to sea."
And 'e went, for I 'adn't broke 'is will,
  Though God knows 'ow I tried,
And 'e never set eyes on my face again
  Till the day as 'is mother died.
Well, maybe that's 'ow it is wi' God,
  'Is sons 'ave got to be free;
Their wills are their own, and their lives their own,
  And that's 'ow it 'as to be.
So the Father God goes sorrowing still
  For 'Is world what 'as gone to sea,
But 'E runs up a light on Calvary's 'eight
  That beckons to you and me.
The beacon light of the sorrow of God
  'As been shinin' down the years,
A-flashin' its light through the darkest night
  O' our 'uman blood and tears.
There's a sight o' things what I thought was strange,
  As I'm just beginnin' to see:
"Inasmuch as ye did it to one of these
  Ye 'ave done it unto Me."
So it isn't just only the crown o' thorns
  What 'as pierced and torn God's 'ead;
'E knows the feel uv a bullet, too,
  And 'E's 'ad 'Is touch o' the lead.
And 'E's standin' wi' me in this 'ere sap,
  And the corporal stands wiv 'Im,
And the eyes of the laddie is shinin' bright,
  But the eyes of the Christ burn dim.
O' laddie, I thought as ye'd done for me
  And broke my 'eart wi' your pain.
I thought as ye'd taught me that God were dead,
  But ye've brought 'Im to life again.
And ye've taught me more of what God is
  Than I ever thought to know,

For I never thought 'E could come so close
   Or that I could love 'Im so.
For the voice of the Lord, as I 'ears it now,
   Is the voice of my pals what bled,
And the call of my country's God to me
   Is the call of my country's dead.

WELL?

Our Padre were a solemn bloke,
   We called 'im dismal Jim.
It fairly gave ye t' bloomin' creeps,
   To sit and 'ark at 'im,
When 'e were on wi' Judgment Day,
   Abaht that great white throne,
And 'ow each chap would 'ave to stand,
   And answer on 'is own.
And if 'e tried to charnce 'is arm,
   And 'ide a single sin,
There'd be the angel Gabriel,
   Wi' books to do 'im in.
'E 'ad it all writ dahn, 'e said,
   And nothin' could be 'id,
'E 'ad it all i' black and white,
   And 'E would take no kid.
And every single idle word,
   A soldier charnced to say,
'E'd 'ave it all thrown back at 'im,
   I' court on Judgment Day.
Well I kep' mindin' Billy Briggs,
   A pal o' mine what died.
'E went to 'elp our sergeant Smith,
   But as 'e reached 'is side,

120

There came and bust atween 'is legs,
    A big Boche 5·9 pill.
And I picked up 'is corpril's stripes,
    That's all there were o' Bill.
I called to mind a stinkin' night
    When we was carryin' tea.
We went round there by Limerick Lane,
    And Bill were a'ead o' me.
'Twere rainin' 'eavens 'ard, ye know,
    And t' boards were thick wi' muck,
And umpteen times we slithered dahn,
    And got the dicksee stuck.
Well, when we got there by the switch,
    A loose board tipped right up,
And Bill, 'e turned a somersault,
    And dahn 'e came, and whup!
I've 'eard men blind, I've 'eard 'em cuss,
    And I've 'eard 'em do it 'ard;
Well, 'aven't I 'eard our R.S.M.,
    Inspectin' special guard!
But Bill, 'e left 'im standin' still.
    'E turned the black night blue,
And I guess the angel Gabriel
    'Ad short 'and work to do.
Well, 'ow would poor old Bill go on,
    When 'e stood all alone,
And 'ad to 'ear that tale read out
    Afore the great white throne?
If what our Padre says is right,
    'E'd 'ave a rotten spell,
And finish up uv it, I s'pose,
    'E'd 'ave to go to 'ell.
And yet 'e were a decent lad,
    And met a decent end;
You'll never finish decenter,
    Than tryin' to 'elp a friend.

But some'ow I can't think it's right,
    It ain't what God would do.
This stunt of all these record books,
    I think it's all napoo,
'Twould let some rotten beggars in,
    And keep some good 'uns out,
There's lots o' blokes, what does no wrong,
    As can't do nowt but shout.
But t'other night I dreamed a dream,
    And, just 'twixt me and you,
I never dreamed like that afore:
    I 'arf thinks it were true.
I dreamed as I were dead, ye see,
    At least as I 'ad died,
For I were very much alive,
    Out there on t'other side.
I couldn't see no judgment court,
    Nor yet that white great throne,
I couldn't see no record books,
    I seemed to stand alone.
I seemed to stand alone, beside
    A solemn kind o' sea.
Its waves they got in my inside,
    And touched my memory,
And day by day, and year by year,
    My life came back to me.
I seed just what I were, and what
    I'd 'ad the charnce to be.
And all the good I might 'a' done,
    And 'adn't stopped to do.
I seed I'd made an 'ash of it,
    And Gawd! but it were true.
A throng o' faces came and went,
    Afore me on that shore,
My wife, and mother, kiddies, pals,
    And the face of a London whore.

And some was sweet, and some was sad,
    And some put me to shame,
For the dirty things I'd done to 'em,
    When I 'adn't played the game.
Then in the silence some one stirred,
    Like when a sick man groans,
And a kind o' shivering chill ran through
    The marrer uv my bones.
And there before me some one stood,
    Just lookin' dahn at me,
And still be'ind 'Im moaned and moaned
    That everlastin' sea.
I couldn't speak, I felt as though
    'E 'ad me by the throat,
'Twere like a drownin' fellah feels,
    Last moment 'e's afloat.
And 'E said nowt, 'E just stood still
    For I dunno 'ow long.
It seemed to me like years and years,
    But time out there's all wrong.
"What was 'E like?" you're askin' now.
    Can't word it anyway,
'E just were 'Im, that's all I knows.
    There's things as words can't say.
It seemed to me as though 'Is face
    Were millions rolled in one;
It never changed yet always changed,
    Like the sea beneath the sun.
'Twere all men's face yet no man's face,
    And a face no man can see,
And it seemed to say in silent speech,
    "Ye did 'em all to Me.
The dirty things ye did to 'em,
    The filth ye thought was fine,
Ye did 'em all to Me," it said,
    "For all their souls were Mine."

All eyes was in 'Is eyes—all eyes,
    My wife's and a million more;
And once I thought as those two eyes
    Were the eyes of the London whore.
And they was sad—my Gawd, 'ow sad,
    Wiv tears what seemed to shine,
And quivering bright wi' the speech o' light
    They said, "'Er soul was Mine."
And then at last 'E said one word,
    'E just said one word—"Well?"
And I said in a funny voice,
    "Please can I go to 'Ell?"
And 'E stood there and looked at me,
    And 'E kind o' seemed to grow,
Till 'E shone like the sun above my 'ead,
    And then 'E answered "No,
You can't, that 'Ell is for the blind,
    And not for those that see.
You know that you 'ave earned it, lad,
    So you must follow Me.
Follow Me on by the paths o' pain,
    Seeking what you 'ave seen,
Until at last you can build the 'Is'
    Wi' the brick o' the 'Might 'ave been.'"
That's what 'E said, as I'm alive,
    And that there dream were true.
But what 'E meant—I don't quite know,
    Though I knows what I 'as to do.
I's got to follow what I's seen,
    Till this old carcass dies;
For I daren't face in the land o' grace
    The sorrow o' those eyes.
There ain't no throne, and there ain't no books,
    It's 'Im you've got to see,
It's 'Im, just 'Im, that is the Judge
    Of blokes like you and me.

And, boys, I'd sooner frizzle up,
    I' the flames of a burnin' 'Ell,
Than stand and look into 'Is face,
    And 'ear 'Is voice say — *"Well?"*

THE SECRET

You were askin' 'ow we sticks it,
    Sticks this blarsted rain and mud,
'Ow it is we keeps on smilin'
    When the place runs red wi' blood.
Since you're askin', I can tell ye,
    And I thinks I tells ye true,
But it ain't official, mind ye,
    It's a tip 'twixt me and you.
For the General thinks it's tactics,
    And the bloomin' plans 'e makes;
And the C.O. thinks it's trainin',
    And the trouble as he takes.
Sargint-Major says it's drillin',
    And 'is straffin' on parade;
Doctor swears it's sanitation,
    And some patent stinks 'e's made.
Padre tells us it's religion,
    And the Spirit of the Lord;
But I ain't got much religion,
    And I sticks it still, by Gawd.
Quarters kids us it's the rations,
    And the dinners as we gets;
But I knows what keeps us smilin',
    It's the Woodbine Cigarettes.
For the daytime seems more dreary,
    And the night-time seems to drag

To eternity of darkness,
   When ye 'aven't got a fag.
Then the rain seems some'ow wetter,
   And the cold cuts twice as keen,
And ye keeps on seein' Boches,
   What the Sargint 'asn't seen.
If ole Fritz 'as been and got ye,
   And ye 'ave to stick the pain,
If ye 'aven't got a fag on,
   Why, it 'urts as bad again.
When there ain't no fags to pull at,
   Then there's terror in the ranks.
That's the secret—(yes, I'll 'ave one)
   Just a fag—and many Tanks.

WHAT'S THE GOOD?

Well, I've done my bit o' scrappin',
   And I've done in quite a lot;
Nicked 'em neatly wiv my bayonet,
   So I needn't waste a shot.
'Twas my duty, and I done it,
   But I 'opes the doctor's quick,
For I wish I 'adn't done it;
   Gawd! it turns me shamed and sick.

There's a young 'un like our Richard,
   And I bashed 'is 'ead in two,
And there's that ole grey-'aired geezer
   Which I stuck 'is belly through.
Gawd, you women, wives, and mothers,
   It's sich waste of all your pain!
If you knowed what I'd been doin',
   Could yer kiss me still, my Jane?

When I sets me dahn to tell yer
    What it means to scrap and fight,
Could I tell ye true and honest,
    Make ye see this bleedin' sight?
No, I couldn't and I wouldn't,
    It would turn your 'air all grey;
Women suffers 'ell to bear us,
    And we suffers 'ell to slay.
I suppose some Fritz went courtin'
    In the gloamin' same as me,
And the old world turned to 'eaven
    When they kissed beneath a tree.
And each evening seemed more golden,
    Till the day as they was wed,
And 'is bride stood shy and blushin',
    Like a June rose, soft and red.
I remembers 'ow it were, lass,
    On that silver night in May,
When ye 'ung your 'ead and whispered
    That ye couldn't say me nay.
Then, when June brought in the roses,
    And you changed your maiden name,
'Ow ye stood there, shy and blushin',
    When the call uv evening came.
I remembers 'ow I loved ye,
    When ye arsked me in your pride
'Ow I'd liked my Sunday dinner
    As ye nestled at my side.
For between a thousand races
    Lands may stretch and seas may foam,

But it makes no bloomin' difference,
    Boche or Briton, 'ome is 'ome.
I remember what 'e cost ye,
    When I gave ye up for dead,

As I 'eld your 'and and watched ye
   With the little lad in bed.

'Struth, I wish 'e'd stop 'is lookin',
   And shut up 'is bloomin' eyes.
'Cause I keeps on seein' Richard
   When I whacks 'im and 'e cries.
Damn the blasted war to 'ell, lass,
   It's just bloody rotten waste;
Them as gas on war and glory
   Oughter come and 'ave a taste.
Yes, I larned what women suffers
   When I seed you stand the test,
But you knowed as it were worth it
   When 'e felt to find your breast.
All your pain were clean forgotten
   When you touched 'is little 'ead,
And ye sat up proud and smilin',
   Wiv a living lad in bed.
But we suffers too—we suffers,
   Like the damned as groans in 'ell,
And we 'aven't got no babies,
   Only mud, and blood, and smell.
'Tain't the suff'rin' as I grouse at,
   I can stick my bit o' pain;
But I keeps on allus askin'
   What's the good, and who's to gain?
When ye've got "a plain objective"
   Ye can fight your fight and grin,
But there ain't no damned objective,
   And there ain't no prize to win.
We're just like a lot o' bullocks
   In a blarsted china shop,
Bustin' all the world to blazes,
   'Cause we dunno 'ow to stop,

Trampling years of work and wonder
    Into dust beneath our feet,
And the one as does most damage
    Swears that victory is sweet.
It's a sweet as turns to bitter,
    Like the bitterness of gall,
And the winner knows 'e's losin'
    If 'e stops to think at all.
I suppose this ain't the spirit
    Of the Patriotic man;
Didn't ought to do no thinkin';
    Soldiers just kill all they can.
But we carn't 'elp thinkin' sometimes,
    Though our business is to kill,
War 'as turned us into butchers,
    But we're only 'uman still.
Gawd knows well I ain't no thinker,
    And I never knew before,
But I knows now why I'm fightin',
    It's to put an end to war.
Not to make my country richer,
    Or to keep her flag unfurled
Over every other nation,
    Tyrant mistress of the world.
Not to boast of Britain's glory,
    Bought by bloodshed in her wars,
But that Peace may shine about her,
    As the sea shines round her shores.
If ole Fritz believes in fightin',
    And obeys 'is War Lord's will,
Well, until 'e stops believin',
    It's my job to fight and kill.
But the Briton ain't no butcher,
    'E's a peaceful cove at 'eart,
And it's only 'cause 'e 'as to,
    That 'e plays the butcher's part.

'Cause I 'as to—that's the reason
　　Why I done the likes o' this;
You're an understanding woman,
　　And you won't refuse your kiss.
Women pity soldiers' sorrow,
　　That can bring no son to birth,
Only death and devastation,
　　Darkness over all the earth.
We won't 'ave no babe to cuddle,
　　Like a blessing to the breast.
We'll just 'ave a bloody mem'ry
　　To disturb us when we rest.
But the kids will some day bless us,
　　When they grows up British men,
'Cause we tamed the Prussian tyrant,
　　And brought Peace to earth again.

OLD ENGLAND

Yes, I'm fightin' for old England
　　And for eighteenpence a day,
And I'm fightin' like an 'ero,
　　So the daily papers say.
Well, I ain't no downy chicken,
　　I'm a bloke past forty-three,
And I'm goin' to tell ye honest
　　What old England means to me.
When I joined the British Army
　　I'd bin workin' thirty years,
But I left my bloomin' rent-book
　　Showin' three months in arrears.
No, I weren't no chronic boozer,
　　Nor I weren't a lad to bet;

I worked 'ard when I could get it,
  And I weren't afeared to sweat.
But I weren't a tradesman proper,
  And the work were oft to seek,
So the most as I could addle
  Were abaht a quid a week.
And when me and Jane got married,
  And we 'ad our oldest kid,
We soon learned 'ow many shillings
  Go to make a golden quid.
For we 'ad to keep our clubs up,
  And there's three and six for rent,
And with food and boots and clothing
  It no sooner came than went.
Then when kiddies kep' on comin'—
  We reared four and buried three;
My ole woman couldn't do it,
  So we got in debt—ye see.
And we 'ad a 'eap o' sickness
  And we got struck off the club,
With our little lot o' troubles
  We just couldn't pay the sub.
No, I won't tell you no false'oods;
  There were times I felt that queer,
That I went and did the dirty,
  And I 'ad a drop o' beer.
Then the wife and me 'ud quarrel,
  And our 'ome were little 'ell,
Wiv the 'ungry kiddies cryin',
  Till I eased up for a spell.
There were times when it were better,
  And some times when it were worse,
But to take it altogether,
  My old England were a curse.
It were sleepin', sweatin', starvin',
  Wearing boot soles for a job.

It were sucking up to foremen
  What 'ud sell ye for a bob.
It were cringin', crawlin', whinin',
  For the right to earn your bread,
It were schemin', pinchin', plannin',
  It were wishin' ye was dead.
I'm not fightin' for old England,
  Not for this child—am I? 'Ell!
For the sake o' that old England
  I'd not face a single shell,
Not a single bloomin' whizzbang.
  Never mind this blarsted show,
With your comrades fallin' round ye,
  Lyin' bleedin' in a row.
This ain't war, it's ruddy murder,
  It's a stinkin' slaughter 'ouse.
'Ark to that one, if 'e got ye
  'E'd just squash ye like this louse.
Would I do this for old England,
  Would I? 'Ell, I says, not me!
What I says is, sink old England
  To the bottom of the sea!
It's new England as I fights for,
  It's an England swep' aht clean,
It's an England where we'll get at
  Things our eyes 'ave never seen;
Decent wages, justice, mercy,
  And a chance for ev'ry man
For to make 'is 'ome an 'eaven
  If 'e does the best 'e can.
It's that better, cleaner England,
  Made o' better, cleaner men,
It's that England as I fights for,
  And I'm game to fight again.
It's the better land o' Blighty
  That still shines afore our eyes,

That's the land a soldier fights for,
 And for that a soldier dies.

THE SNIPER

There's a Jerry over there, Sarge!
Can't you see 'is big square 'ead?
If 'e bobs it up again there,
I'll soon nail 'im — nail 'im dead.
Gimme up that pair o' glasses,
And just fix that blinkin' sight.
Gawd! that nearly almost got 'im,
There 'e is now — see? 'Arf right.
If 'e moves again I'll get 'im,
Take these glasses 'ere and see,
What's that? Got 'im through the 'ead, Sarge?
Where's my blarsted cup o' tea?

PASSING THE LOVE OF
WOMEN

Yes, I've sat in the summer twilight,
 Wiv a nice girl, 'and in 'and,
But I've thought even then of the shell 'oles,
 Where the boys of the old Bat. stand.
I've turned to 'er lips for 'er kisses,
 And I've found them kisses cold,
Stone cold and pale like a twice-told tale,
 What has gorn all stale and old.
And the light in 'er eyes 'as gorn all faint,
 And the sound of 'er voice grown dim,

As I 'eard the machine-guns singin' aht,
  A-singin' their evenin' 'ymn.
Yes, I've known the love uv a woman, lad,
  And maybe I shall again,
But I knows a stronger love than theirs,
  And that is the love of men.
I could keep my cushy billet, lad,
  If I liked to swing the lead,
I could kiss my gal in the gloamin',
  And sleep in a decent bed.
But I've 'eard my comrades callin' aht,
  From across that bit uv sea.
"Come back — come back — would ye loaf and slack,
  And leave it to such as we?
Come back — come back" — with their old tack-tack,
  I can 'ear the machine-guns sing,
"Come back — come back — don't skunk and slack,
  For this ain't no time to swing;
Come back — come back into No Man's Land,
  For that is the land of men,
And No Man's Land is the true man's land,
  Come back — come back again."
Ay, the love of women draws ye, lad,
  It's the oldest, sweetest spell,
But your comrade Love is stronger love,
  'Cause it draws ye back to 'ell.
The love of a woman draws to 'eaven,
  An 'eaven of 'uman bliss,
To the eyes that sing, the arms that cling,
  And the long, long lovers' kiss.
But your comrades keep on callin' ye,
  Callin' ye back to 'ell,
To the fear o' death and the chokin' breath,
  Drawn thick with a sickly smell.
Gawd knows, old sport, I 'ave loved my lass
  As a man should love his mate,

Body and soul I 'ave loved my lass,
    But this love's strong—like Fate.
It 'as cut down deep, to see 'er weep,
    And she knows I love 'er well,
But I must go back to the old tack-tack,
    To my pals and to Bloody 'Ell.

PRAYER BEFORE AN ATTACK

It ain't as I 'opes 'E'll keep me safe
    While the other blokes goes down,
It ain't as I wants to leave this world
    And wear an 'ero's crown.
It ain't for that as I says my prayers
    When I goes to the attack,
But I pray that whatever comes my way
    I may never turn me back.
I leaves the matter o' life and death
    To the Father who knows what's best,
And I prays that I still may play the man
    Whether I turns east or west.
I'd sooner that it were east, ye know,
    To Blighty and my gal Sue;
I'd sooner be there, wi' the gold in 'er 'air,
    And the skies be'ind all blue.
But still I pray I may do my bit,
    And then, if I must turn west,
I'll be unashamed when my name is named.
    And I'll find a soldier's rest.

Easy does it—bit o' trench 'ere,
Mind that blinkin' bit o' wire,
There's a shell 'ole on your left there,
Lift 'im up a little 'igher.
Stick it, lad, ye'll soon be there now,
Want to rest 'ere for a while?
Let 'im dahn then—gently—gently,
There ye are, lad.   That's the style.
Want a drink, mate?   'Ere's my bottle,
Lift 'is 'ead up for 'im, Jack,
Put my tunic underneath 'im,
'Ow's that, chummy?   That's the tack!
Guess we'd better make a start now,
Ready for another spell?
Best be goin', we won't 'urt ye,
But 'e might just start to shell.
Are ye right, mate?   Off we goes then.
That's well over on the right;
Gawd Almighty, that's a near 'un!
'Old your end up good and tight,
Never mind, lad, you're for Blighty.
Mind this rotten bit o' board.
We'll soon 'ave ye tucked in bed, lad,
'Opes ye gets to my old ward.
No more war for you, my 'earty,
This'll get ye well away,
Twelve good months in dear old Blighty,
Twelve good months if you're a day.
M.O.'s got a bit o' something
What'll stop that blarsted pain.
'Ere's a rotten bit o' ground, mate,
Lift up 'igher—up again,

Wish 'e'd stop 'is blarsted shellin',
Makes it rotten for the lad.
When a feller's been and got it,
It affec's 'im twice as bad.
'Ow's it goin' now then, sonny?
'Ere's that narrow bit o' trench,
Careful, mate, there's some dead Jerries.
Gawd Almighty, what a stench!
'Ere we are now, stretcher-case, boys,
Bring him aht a cup o' tea!
Inasmuch as ye have done it
Ye have done it unto Me.

TO-DAY THOU SHALT BE
WITH ME

Gawd! 'ow it shoots!
From my 'ead to my boots!
And back to my 'ead again!
You never can tell,
But I don't think 'ell
Can be worse than this blarsted pain.

There's 'eaven and 'ell,
They say so—well,
I dunno what they mean,
But it's touch and go,
And I may soon know;
It's funny there's nothin' between.

I've drunk and I've swore,
And the girl next door
Is a' breakin' 'er 'eart thro' me.

137

She's a bonny lass—
Gawd damn this gas!
I wonder just where I'll be.

I remembers a day,
When they blazed away,
And they bust up a church to bits:
But the cross still stood,
It were only wood.
This pain—it's givin' me fits.

Ay, there it stands,
With its outstretched hands,
And I can't 'elp wonderin' why.
I can't quite see,
Is 'E lookin' at me?
O Gawd, am I goin' to die!

I can't! Not yet!
My Gawd, I sweat!
There's a mist comin' over my eyes.
Christ, let me be,
To-day, with Thee.
You took a *thief* to Paradise!

NO RETALIATION

There's another gorn to glory!
Damn and blast these blinkin' 'Uns!
Where's our damn retaliation?
What's the matter wiv the guns?
If they'd only give 'em rations
Same as they keeps givin' us,
They'd soon stop their bloomin' antics—

Gawd, it makes a fellah cuss.
One by one I sees 'em goin',
All the gamest and the best,
One by one they keeps on goin',
There's another lad gorn west.
I suppose there's no moonitions;
Got to save up for a spell.
While they does their blarsted savin',
My platoon gets blowed to 'ell.
Damn these blame moonition workers,
Damn them and their bloomin' strike,
Thinks it's same as Peace conditions,
They can do just as they like.
Think o' Jimmy Brown! 'E's earnin'
Easy four pun ten a week,
And 'e's struck for better money—
'E's the one as oughter speak—
Been and bought a noo pianer,
And 'is wife a noo fur coat,
Gawd, I 'opes 'is Sunday dinner
Stops and turns round in 'is throat!
'Ow'd 'e like these blarsted trenches?
'Ow'd 'e like this cussed mud?
'Ow'd 'e like 'is Sunday dinner
From a dicksee stained wiv blood?
'Ow'd 'e like to sit and eat it
Next an 'arf unburied Fritz,
Wiv a smell what turns your stummick
As ye eats a bite and spits?
Better money! Gawd Almighty!
Give us sporting charnce uv life.
I don't arsk for better money,
Gimme leave to see my wife.
She don't want no noo pianer,
All she wants is me come 'ome,
If there's no retaliation,

All I gets is kingdom come.
Better money—better money,
Gawd, it makes a fellah sick,
All they thinks abaht is money,
And they makes it too damn quick.
But it's rotten bloody money,
Oughter rob 'em of their sleep,
They're just buyin' British bodies,
Buyin' tears what women weep.
Don't I wish I 'ad 'em 'ere now,
I'd soon teach 'em what is what,
They'd soon strike for better money,
This 'ud touch 'em on the spot.
All the blokes what's on moonitions
Oughter come 'ere for a spell;
All them dudes what's profiteerin'
Oughter be out 'ere—in 'ell.
Gawd, the blighters couldn't do it,
If they damn well only knew;
But they don't—they won't believe it.
They don't think that war is true.

THY WILL BE DONE

A Sermon in a Hospital

I were puzzled about this prayin' stunt,
    And all as the parsons say,
For they kep' on sayin', and sayin',
    And yet it weren't plain no way.
For they told us never to worry,
    But simply to trust in the Lord,
"Ask and ye shall receive," they said,
    And it sounds orlright, but, Gawd!

It's a mighty puzzling business,
    For it don't allus work that way,
Ye may ask like mad, and ye don't receive
    As I found out t'other day.
I were sittin' me down on my 'unkers,
    And 'avin' a pull at my pipe,
And larfin' like fun at a blind old 'Un,
    What were 'avin' a try to snipe.
For 'e couldn't shoot for monkey nuts,
    The blinkin' blear-eyed ass,
So I sits, and I spits, and I 'ums a tune;
    And I never thought o' the gas.
Then all of a suddint I jumps to my feet,
    For I 'eard the strombos sound,
And I pops up my 'ead a bit over the bags
    To 'ave a good look all round.
And there I seed it, comin' across,
    Like a girt big yaller cloud,
Then I 'olds my breath, i' the fear o' death,
    Till I bust, then I prayed aloud.
I prayed to the Lord Almighty above,
    For to shift that blinkin' wind,
But it kep' on blowin' the same old way,
    And the chap next me, 'e grinned.
"It's no use prayin'," 'e said, "let's run,"
    And we fairly took to our 'eels,
But the gas ran faster nor we could run,
    And, Gawd, you know 'ow it feels!
Like a thousand rats and a million chats,
    All tearin' away at your chest,
And your legs won't run, and you're fairly done,
    And you've got to give up and rest.
Then the darkness comes, and ye knows no more
    Till ye wakes in an 'orspital bed.
And some never knows nothin' more at all,
    Like my pal Bill—'e's dead.

Now, 'ow was it 'E didn't shift that wind,
    When I axed in the name o' the Lord?
With the 'orror of death in every breath,
    Still I prayed every breath I drawed.
That beat me clean, and I thought and I thought
    Till I came near bustin' my 'ead.
It weren't.for me I were grieved, ye see,
    It were my pal Bill—'e's dead.
For me, I'm a single man, but Bill
    'As kiddies at 'ome and a wife.
And why ever the Lord didn't shift that wind
    I just couldn't see for my life.
But I've just bin readin' a story 'ere,
    Of the night afore Jesus died,
And of 'ow 'E prayed in Gethsemane,
    'Ow 'E fell on 'Is face and cried.
Cried to the Lord Almighty above
    Till 'E broke in a bloody sweat,
And 'E were the Son of the Lord, 'E were,
    And 'E prayed to 'Im 'ard; and yet,
And yet 'E 'ad to go through wiv it, boys,
    Just same as pore Bill what died.
'E prayed to the Lord, and 'E sweated blood,
    And yet 'E were crucified.
But 'Is prayer were answered, I sees it now,
    For though 'E were sorely tried,
Still 'E went wiv 'Is trust in the Lord unbroke,
    And 'Is soul it were satisfied.
For 'E felt 'E were doin' God's Will, ye see,
    What 'E came on the earth to do,
And the answer what came to the prayers 'E prayed
    Were 'Is power to see it through;
To see it through to the bitter end,
    And to die like a Gawd at the last,
In a glory of light that were dawning bright
    Wi' the sorrow of death all past.

142

And the Christ who was 'ung on the Cross is Gawd,
   True Gawd for me and you,
For the only Gawd that a true man trusts
   Is the Gawd what sees it through.
And Bill, 'e were doin' 'is duty, boys,
   What 'e came on the earth to do,
And the answer what came to the prayers I prayed
   Were 'is power to see it through;
To see it through to the very end,
   And to die as my old pal died,
Wi' a thought for 'is pal and a prayer for 'is gal,
   And 'is brave 'eart satisfied.

WHAT'S THE USE OF A
CROSS TO 'IM?

Parson says I'm to make 'im a cross
   To set up over 'is grave,
'E's buried there by the Moated Grange,
   And I 'ad a damn close shave,
But 'e were taken and I were left,
   And why, it's a job to see,
For 'e 'ad a wife and some bonnie kids,
   And me—well, there's only me.
And what's the use of a cross to 'im?
   'E weren't a religious man,
'E said no prayers and 'e sang no 'ymns—
   I'll make this do if I can.
It's all full o' notches—an awkward piece,
   But I'll see what a knife'll do.
I allus were one to respec' the dead,
   And 'e were a good pal too.
'E weren't a religious man, not 'im,
   Far as that goes—nor am I.

I wonder what odds religion makes
  When a feller comes to die.
It's a curious thing is death, ye know.
  When we was back there at rest,
'E were singin' 'is song—and takin' 'is glass,
  And 'avin' 'is fun wiv the best.
'E weren't no boozer though, mind ye that,
  'E were sound uv 'is wind and limb,
'E were 'ard as a nail—a fighting lad,
  A daisy to scrap were Jim.
But 'e'll fight no more—'e's gorn aht West
  Wiv a great big 'ole in 'is back,
'E's pushin' up daisies by Moated Grange—
  Now where did I put that tack?
I minds me arskin' a hatheist,
  'E were livin' dahn our street,
'E looked like a stick wiv a turnip on,
  But talkin' 'e 'ad me beat.
I minds me arskin' in Railway Inn
  What 'e thought 'appened the dead?
'E took a candle and snuffed it aht,
  "That's what I think," he said.
But some'ow I carn't think that 'ere,
  When a pal gets blowed out West;
I were sure when my poor old mother died,
  She'd gorn to a land o' rest.
I carn't make much o' what parsons say,
  Abaht 'eaven and all them things,
'Eavenly cities wiv gates of pearl,
  An' angels wiv shining wings,
An' I carn't see old pal Jim up there,
  Wiv a golden 'arp in 'is 'and,
A-playin' of 'ymns in a horchestra,
  At 'ome in the angels' band.
'E'd feel that awkward and out o' place,
  And fair fed up for a drink,

If I was by and just catched 'is eye
    I bet 'e'd give me the wink:
"For Gawd's sake bring up a bottle o' Bass,
    Or a barrel o' that French beer;
It's 'orrible dry sittin' up on 'igh
    And singin' these 'ymn toons 'ere!"
'E weren't so bad at a ragtime song,
    But they don't 'ave ragtime there;
If 'e were to tip 'em aht Dixie Land
    'E'd make them angels stare.
But 'e ain't gorn dahn to no 'ell fire,
    'E 'ad a good 'eart, 'ad Jim.
'Is wife were as good as a lump o' gold,
    And she thought the world of 'im.
There must be a place for the likes o' Jim,
    What isn't religious blokes,
But is good to their pals in the trenches,
    And dear to their own 'ome folks.
It must be the same great Gawd above
    What 'as made this world dahn 'ere,
And it takes all sorts to make this world,
    So there ain't no bloomin' fear
But what 'E'll fix up a job for Jim,
    A job what'll suit 'is 'and,
Maybe 'e'll polish them golden 'arps
    They use in the 'eavenly band.

Maybe there's some flowers and gardens there
    What'll want a good 'andy man:
I can just see Jim wiv an angel's spade
    And a 'eavenly wat'ring can.
'E were a gard'ner in civil life,
    'E loved 'is allotment land,
'E were allus potterin' round 'is bit,
    My Gawd—but it did smell grand.

'E 'ad rhubarb, cabbage, and radishes,
　　Fit for a prize at the shows,
Pansies and daisies and mignonette,
　　And that great big summer rose.
Many a Sunday I've sat wiv 'im,
　　And 'ad a good pull at my pipe—
My Gawd, them days!　It's a bloody war—
　　Where 'ave I put my wipe?
Ay, there we'd sit and we'd chew the rag
　　And 'ark to the church bells ring,
'Twere Sunday there—wiv the spring in the air,
　　And Peace over everything.

Blyme, I wants no 'eaven but that
　　In the land o' the Kingdom come,
A pal and a pipe and a garden there—
　　Ugh! damn it, I've 'it my thumb.
There, I've finished 'is bit of a cross,
　　It's a rough-looking awkward thing,
But it's all I can do with this wood, old lad—
　　Just 'ark 'ow them church bells ring!
I can 'ear 'em soundin' across the sea
　　From the land where 'is garden grows,
I can see the green uv them cabbages,
　　And smell the smell uv that rose.
Gawd knows as I ain't no prayin' man,
　　But I just puts up this prayer:
If Ye're stuck for a job what'll suit old Jim,
　　Lord, give 'im a garden there,
And then when it comes my turn to go,
　　Just put me along of 'im.
I know as I ain't fit for 'eaven,
　　But gimme a job wiv Jim,
In a garden just outside the gates,
　　Where the 'eavenly roses smells,

146

And blokes what ain't quite fit for 'eaven
  Can 'ark to the 'eavenly bells.

I KNOW NOT WHERE THEY
HAVE LAID HIM

I wouldn't mind if I only knowed
  The spot where they'd laid my lad;
If I could see where they'd buried 'im,
  It wouldn't be arf so bad.
But they do say some's not buried at all,
  Left to the maggots and flies,
Rottin' out there in that no man's land,
  Just where they falls—they lies.
Parson 'e says as it makes no odds,
  'Cause the soul o' the lad goes on,
'Is spirit 'as gorn to 'is Gawd, 'e says,
  Wherever 'is body 'as gorn.
But Parson ain't never 'ad no child,
  'E's a man, not a woman, see?
'Ow can 'e know what a woman feels,
  And what it can mean to me?
For my boy's body were mine—my own,
  I bore it in bitter pain,
Bone of my bone and flesh of my flesh,
  It lies and rots in the rain.
Parson ain't never suckled a child,
  Nor broken 'is nights o' rest,
To 'ush it to sleep in 'is aching arms,
  While it drew life from 'is breast.
'E ain't never watched by a sick child's bed,
  Nor seed it fightin' for life;
A man don't know what a mother knows,
  'E leaves all that to 'is wife.

I minds that chapter as Parson read
    When poor little Jenny died,
And I were feeling as I feel now,
    Wiv this emptiness inside.
Thou fool—it said—thou fool—for to ask
    And 'ow do the dead arise?
What is the body that they shall wear
    Up there in God's Paradise?
I may be a fool, but that's just it,
    That's just what I wants to know,
What is the body my boy shall bear,
    And 'ow does that body grow?
I reckons as 'ow that Scripture piece
    Were writ by a single man;
They never knows what a body costs,
    And I don't see 'ow they can.
A married man 'as a bit uv sense
    If 'e's been and stood wiv 'is wife,
'E knows the body 'is baby wears
    'As cost 'er all but 'er life.
But even a father never knows
    The ache in a mother's 'eart,
When she and the body 'er body bore
    Are severed and torn apart.
The men wouldn't make these cursed wars
    If they knowed of a body's worth,
They wouldn't be blowin' 'em all to bits
    If they 'ad the pains uv birth.
But bless ye—the men don't know they're born,
    For they gets away scot-free.
'Ow can they know what their cruel wars
    Is costin' the likes uv me?
I were proud to give, I'd give again
    If I knowed the cause were right,
For I wouldn't keep no son of mine
    When 'is dooty called to fight.

But I'd like to know just where it's laid,
    That body my body bore,
And I'd like to know who'll mother 'im
    Out there on that other shore,
Who will be bearin' the mother's part
    And be makin' your body, boy?
Who will be 'avin' the mother's pain,
    And feelin' the mother's joy?
Gawd, is it you?   Then bow You down
    And 'ark to a mother's prayer.
Don't keep it all to yourself, Good Lord,
    But give 'is old mother a share.
Gimme a share of the travail pain
    Of my own son's second birth,
Double the pain if you double the joy
    That a mother feels on earth.
Gimme the sorrow and not the joy,
    If that 'as to be Your will;
Gimme the labour and not the pride,
    But make me 'is mother still.
Maybe the body as 'e shall wear
    Is born of my breaking heart,
Maybe these pains are the new birth pangs
    What'll give my laddie 'is start.
Then I'd not trouble 'ow hard they was,
    I'd gladly go through the mill,
If that noo body 'e wore were mine,
    And I were 'is mother still.

O'GRADY'S LETTER

(With Apologies to the Author of "The Mountains of Mourne")

Dear Mary, I've comed to a wonderful shpot,
And I wish I could stop here, but fear I cannot;

It's quiet and paceful and far from the guns,
And I can't even smell the damn stink of dead Huns;
I slapes in a bed, and I slapes all the night,
And I don't wake in terror of having a fight.
There's only one place where I'd far rather be,
Where the mountains o' Mourne sweep down to the
    sea.

There's beautiful girls here, and though they are French,
Faith, it does your heart good just to see a fine wench,
But that needn't make any diff'rence to you,
For I parle Français pas beaucoup un peu,
And when I comes askin' for one dacent hug,
They say—mais vous avez beaucoup ugly mug.
So if I wants kissin' I'd far better be
Where the mountains o' Mourne sweep down to the sea.

There's some English girls here, we call 'em the
    W.A.A.C.'s,
And they're togged up in khaki, wi' leggin's and macs.
There's nothin' they can't do, and faith you should see
These maidens do drillin' as smart as can be.
And if I weren't faithful, my colleen, to you,
Sure I know what this boy would be tryin' to do!
For I'd do very well wid a W.A.A.C. on each knee,
Where the mountains o' Mourne sweep down to the sea.

We've beaucoup Instructors wid voices like guns,
And wid murderous faces to frighten the Huns,
They makes us look ugly and tells us to swear;
I never was handsome, but now I declare
I spits and I swears when I turns in my bed,
And I strikes the next feller and grins when he's dead;
I've got such a mug that ye'd tremble at me,
Where the mountains o' Mourne sweep down to the sea.

Dear Mary, I tries very hard to be true,
But these French girls is out for to win me from you.
I'm gettin' so good at the French, do ye see,
That begorrah they're always a-chasin' of me.
I met one last night, and I just said "Bon soir,"
And she said, "Voulez-vous promenade avec moi."
If I'm still to be yours, I must hurry, cherie,
Where the mountains o' Mourne sweep down to the sea.

We went for a ride on an automobus,
And, dear Lord, I can tell ye it was fine for us!
We went to a city whose name I can't tell,
And we strolled in the streets and looked round us, and
    well!
I never did see so much powder and puff,
These French damosels is the divil's hot stuff.
But still I remembered ye waitin' for me,
Where the mountains o' Mourne sweep down to the sea.

WORRY

Right as ninepence, thank ye kindly,
    There are umpty worse than me,
I'd be fit to fight to-morrer
    If my bloomin' eyes could see.
But they can't, sir, that's the noosance,
    I'm as blind as forty bats,
And I 'as to work by feel, sir,
    Like ye does at night for chats.
'Ow it 'appened?—well it 'appened
    On a bloomin' night patrol,

When I got a blinkin' whizzbang
  To myself and got it whole.
Yes, the last thing as I seed, sir,
  Were a burst of silver light,
And it went and left the darkness,
  'Cause it took away my sight.
There was me and old Bill Drury
  And 'e got one through the 'ead;
We tried 'ard to fetch 'im back, sir,
  But it weren't no bon—'e's dead.
And it's when I thinks of 'im, sir,
  Uv 'is kiddies and 'is wife,
That I thanks the One above, sir,
  That I still 'ave got my life.
There are times I wants to see, sir,
  Like a beggar wants a meal,
But when I remembers Billie,
  Then I ain't disposed to squeal.
For I've got my legs and arms, sir,
  And these 'ands is willing still,
I can do my job of work yet;
  I can do it—and I will.
There's just one thing I'm afeared on,
  Will they find me work to do?
That's the thing as makes me worry,
  Same as it would worry you.
When this blarsted war is over,
  And we settles dahn again
To the makin' of the money,
  Will they still remember then?
Yes, I know they've been and promised,
  But it's easy to forget.
When the shoutin's done and over,
  There's accounts to settle yet.
There'll be thousands same as me, sir,
  Out to do what work they can,

Not disabled, but like me, sir,
   Not just everybody's man.
Will they find us jobs to work at
   Where two 'ands can earn their pay,
For a wage enough to keep us
   Free from debt, and pay our way?
That's the only thing as worries
   When I sits me down to think,
Will I get my charnce of 'ome, sir,
   And enough to eat and drink?

THE PENSIONER

'Im and me was kids together,
   Played together, went to school,
Where Miss Jenkins used to rap us
   On our knuckles wiv a rule.
When we left we worked together,
   At the Fact'ry, makin' jam,
Gawd 'ave mercy on us women!
   I'm full up to-day—I am.
Well I minds the August Monday,
   When 'e said 'e loved me true,
Underneath the copper beech tree,
   With the moonbeams shining through.
Then we walked down by the River,
   Silent-like an' 'and in 'and,
Till we came there by the Ketch Inn,
   Where them two big willows stand
There 'e caught me roughly to 'im,
   And 'is voice was 'oarse and wild,
As 'e whispered through 'is kisses,
   "Will ye mother me my child?"

An' I took and kissed and kissed 'im,
 Sweet as love and long as life,
Vowed while breath was in my body
 I would be 'is faithful wife.
An' I seemed to see 'is baby,
 Smiling as 'e lay at rest,
With 'is tiny 'and a-clutching
 At the softness of my breast.
Gawd above, them days was 'eaven!
 I can see the river shine
Like a band of silver ribbon;
 I can feel 'is 'and in mine,
I can feel them red 'ot kisses
 On my lips or on my 'air,
I can feel 'is arm tight round me,
 Gawd! I tell ye it ain't fair.
Look ye what the war's done at 'im,
 Lying there as still as death.
See 'is mouth all screwed and twisted,
 With the pain of drawing breath!
But of course I 'ave a pension,
 Coming reg'lar ev'ry week.
So I ain't got much to grouse at—
 I suppose it's like my cheek,
Grousin' when a grateful country
 Buys my food and pays my rent.
I should be most 'umbly grateful
 That my John was one as went,
Went to fight for King and Country,
 Like a 'ero and a man,
I should be most 'umbly grateful,
 And just do as best I can.
But my pension won't buy kisses,
 An' 'e'll never kiss again,
'E ain't got no kissin' in 'im,
 Ain't got nothin' now—but pain.

Not as I would ever change 'im
   For the strongest man alive.
While the breath is in my body
   Still I'll mother 'im—and strive
That I keeps my face still smiling,
   Though my 'eart is fit to break;
As I lives a married widow,
   So I'll live on for 'is sake.
But I says—Let them as makes 'em
   Fight their wars and mourn their dead,
Let their women sleep for ever
   In a loveless, childless bed.
No—I know—it ain't right talkin',
   But there's times as I am wild.
Gawd! you dunno 'ow I wants it—
   'Ow I wants—a child—'is child.

A GAL OF THE STREETS

Verily I say unto you, the . . . harlots go into the Kingdom of
Heaven before you

I met 'er one night down in Leicester Square,
With paint on 'er lips and dye on 'er 'air,
With 'er fixed glad eye and 'er brazen stare—
   She were a gal on the streets.

I was done with leave—on my way to France,
To the ball of death and the devil's dance;
I was raving mad—and glad of the chance
   To meet a gal on the streets.

I went with 'er 'ome—to the cursèd game,
And we talked of men with the talk of shame;
I 'appened to mention a dead pal's name,
   She were a gal on the streets.

"Your pal! Do you know 'im?" she stopped and
        said:
"'Ow is 'e? Where is 'e? I once knowed Ted."
I stuttered and stammered aht—"'E's gorn—dead."
        She were a gal on the streets.

She stood there and swayed like a drunken man,
And 'er face went green where 'er paint began,
Then she muttered, "My Gawd, I carn't"; and ran—
        She were a gal on the streets.

IT'S THE PLUCK

Jesus kept on saying:
Father, forgive them, they know not what they do.

I don't un'erstand religion, but I un'erstands a Man,
    And I'm pretty well aware what men can do,
        I've tramped the whole world over,
        Through 'Frisco back to Dover,
    And I knows my 'uman nature through and through.

Yes, I've done a bit uv scrappin', and I've seen men cuss and
        die,
    And I wouldn't like to write what I 'ave seen,
        For a shell goes anywheres,
        And it don't mind what it tears,
    Leaving lumps of bloody flesh where men 'ave been.

But this tale fair takes the cake; it's a corker, no mistake.
    I can un'erstand them 'oles in 'ands and feet,
        It's a nasty, tender spot
        Where ye gets it good and 'ot,
    For the nerves goes winding round the place, and
        meet

156

Where the nails went in, and, Crikey! but it 'urts, you bet it
         does!
    And it must 'ave 'urt 'Im 'ard as any 'ell;
        For to give ye proper jip,
        'Ell on earth, and no damn lip,
    Why, I'd back them rusty nails agin a shell.

I can un'erstand 'Is stickin' it, and grittin' on 'Is teeth
    For to keep 'Isself from cussin' wiv 'Is lips,
        'Cos the best of blokes is still
        When they've got about their fill,
    And the white man doesn't splutter when 'e grips.

But to pray for them as did it! That's the bit as 'as me
         beat,
    It's away beyond the reach uv mortal men.
        To stick it is the limit,
        No matter 'ow ye trim it,
    This 'ere prayin' is a piece beyond our ken.

Mind ye, I'm not sure I likes it; I'm for giving what ye
         gets—
    I'm for strikin' back as 'ard as you've been struck.
        But I just couldn't do it,
        I'd bust, and blind, and blue it;
    'Tain't the prayin' as I'm gone on—it's the pluck.

THE SPIRIT

When there ain't no gal to kiss you,
And the postman seems to miss you,
And the fags have skipped an issue,
        Carry on.

157

When ye've got an empty belly,
And the "bully's" rotten smelly,
And you're shivering like a jelly,
   Carry on.

When the Boche has done your chum in,
And the sargint's done the rum in,
And there ain't no rations comin',
   Carry on.

When the world is red and reeking,
And the shrapnel shells are shrieking,
And your blood is slowly leaking,
   Carry on.

When the broken, battered trenches
Are like bloody butchers' benches,
And the air is thick with stenches,
   Carry on.

Carry on,
 Though your pals are pale and wan,
And the hope of life is gone,
   Carry on.

For to do more than you can
Is to be a British man,
Not a rotten "also ran"—
   Carry on.